We dedicate this book to all the essential workers around the world who work tirelessly to help the world population fight and survive against the novel coronavirus and similar disease outbreaks.

The 2020 DIY Face Mask Manual

Everything you need to know to protect yourself and your loved ones with DIY face masks and how anyone can make them at home

Patrick Schwientek, PhD
Cheryl A Schwientek
Moritz H von Butler

Warning:
Disease-causing viruses can be very dangerous to life and health. Using face masks, as well as any other instructions provided in this book may be dangerous. It is critical that you follow the advice given by your local government, health authority and licensed professional. If such advice is in dispute with any advice published in this book, disregard the advice published in this book and follow the official advice.

Throughout this book, the above depicted warning icon was used to visually alert the reader about particular risks described in the accompanying text.

Table of Contents

Introduction

There are now more than 2.2 million people infected with COVID-19 worldwide,[1] and researchers at Imperial College London estimate that "in the absence of interventions, COVID-19 would have resulted in 7.0 billion infections and 40 million deaths globally this year."[2] They go on to say that preventive measures "could reduce this burden by half, saving 20 million lives."[2] At the same time, the United States (US) has become the new epicenter of the pandemic: the number of people infected with the virus has surpassed 700,000,[1] and government officials forecast between 100,000–2.2 million deaths in the US alone in the coming months. These are threatening numbers—whichever way they go mainly depends on the measures taken by the government and all of us individually to contain the outbreak.[3]

"In the absence of interventions, COVID-19 would have resulted in 7.0 billion infections and 40 million deaths globally this year."

Imperial College London

As a reaction to these shocking forecasts, governments across the globe have raced to implement strategies to slow down the exponential spread of the outbreak, resulting in half of the 7.8 billion people on the globe now being in coronavirus lockdown.[4] It is generally expected that these suppression measures must be maintained in some manner until vaccines or effective treatments become available—probably no earlier than mid–end of 2021—to avoid further waves of the pandemic.[2] The global lockdown has severe impacts on our social and economic lives: Many people, especially elderly, are completely isolated, and anxiety is high across all income groups.[5]

Unemployment has skyrocketed with the novel coronavirus having already put 17 million Americans out of work in only three weeks and experts expecting these numbers to sharply increase.[6] Many experts suggest we have hit the worst economic recession since the Great Depression, reviving pictures of that time. Many news articles forecast unemployment rates far worse than at the heights of the 2009 financial crisis, which we have just recovered from.[7] To make matters worse, many struggle to even meet their most basic needs. From empty grocery aisles to sold out or unaffordable protective supplies, such as disinfecting cleaners and face masks.

Still, while difficult, we all must follow these preventive measures closely and ensure our family and loved ones follow them as well. Otherwise, we will see even more horrific death tolls than we are already experiencing today.

The key measures recommended by experts from the World Health Organization (WHO), the US Centers for Disease Control and Prevention (CDC), and others, are[8]:

- Maintain social distancing
- Wash hands frequently and avoid touching the face
- Practice good personal and respiratory hygiene
- Seek medical advice immediately if you experience symptoms

A critical additional measure that has already been deployed successfully in Asia from the very beginning of the outbreak is wearing face masks. Until early April of 2020, authorities, such as the CDC and WHO, have debated over the pros and cons of wearing face masks and advised that the general public do not need to wear masks. It is believed this was at least in part driven by the need to preserve medical-grade face masks for healthcare workers, who desperately needed them. The CDC and the US Surgeon General also claimed they feared people would increase hand-to-face contact if advised to use face masks in the general public due to lack of appropriate knowledge and training in their proper use.[9] In particular, surgical masks and N95 respirators were quickly sold out on all major online retailers, soon followed by hand sanitizer and disposable gloves as the disease spread onto more news headlines and media outlets. However, as the numbers of the infected continue to skyrocket in the US and around the globe, many experts have concluded that it is recommended to wear face masks to contain the outbreak and protect yourself and others.

In a press briefing issued on April 3, 2020, it was highlighted that the CDC is now recommending basic cloth or homemade face masks be worn in the general public. This comes in light of studies revealing that the transmission of the novel coronavirus "from individuals without symptoms is playing a more significant role in the spread of the virus than previously understood".[10]

"The CDC is recommending that Americans wear a basic cloth or a fabric mask that can be either purchased online or <u>simply made at home. Probably material that you'd have at home</u>. These face coverings can be easily washed and reused. I want to emphasize that the CDC is not recommending the use of medical-grade or surgical-grade masks[...]"

United States President, Donald Trump

So with evidence proving the potential benefits of wearing face masks in general, such as surgical face masks, the question arises if we all should now go out and compete for the already completely oversold and overpriced medical grade face masks—the ones you have read in the news have increased up to 2,000% in price over these past weeks and are desperately needed by our healthcare workers.

Definitely not, as "medical protective gear must be reserved for the frontline healthcare workers who are performing those vital services".[10] In an unprecedented move, Amazon, the largest US online retailer restricted the sale of these and other critical items to healthcare professionals during this crisis.[11]

Demand for search term "face mask" in the US increased by 1,000%

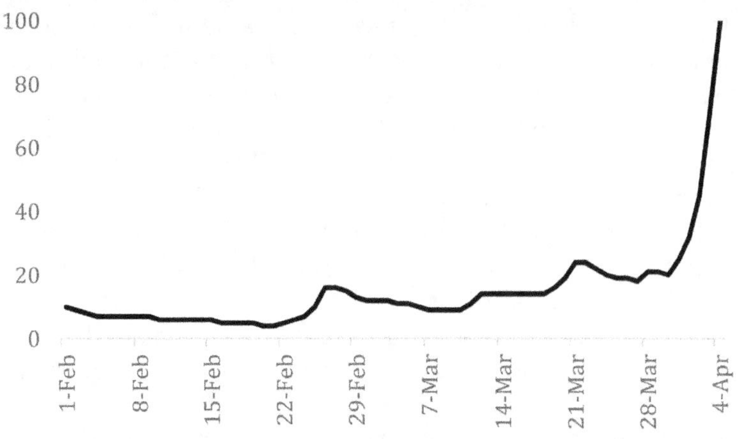

Source: Google Trends search on "face mask", April 4. 2020

This leaves most of us in a dilemma: We now know that wearing face masks is recommended to protect ourselves and our loved ones. At the same time however, we are being told that we must not purchase any of the sparsely available medical grade masks, even if one could afford them after the recent price surge. To make matters worse, most masks are disposable and need to be replaced frequently, racking up even larger costs in keeping up with demand. The run on face masks are also well reflected in Google Trends showing an increase of nearly 1,000% for the search term "face mask". Many scammers exploit the situation and offer completely overpriced or malfunctioning face masks online.

The authors of this book have large families with family members ranging from infants, over kindergarteners up to 95+ aged grandparents. Therefore, protecting ourselves and our loved ones from the novel coronavirus, as well as doing our part in trying to avoid the coronavirus from further spreading is critical for us. At the same time, we are deeply grateful for the selfless dedication with which healthcare workers and essential workers in general put their lives on the line to help those in need and did not want to take away professional face masks from their limited supply. We therefore first set out to make homemade face masks by searching the internet and attempting to following existing guides. We encountered numerous self-help bloggers and YouTubers, as well as newspapers that have picked up on the topic and provide basic descriptions for how to make a face mask at home. While some of these have produced great work,[12,13] we found a lack of well-written, easy to follow and more detailed guides on the topic. Furthermore, during our research on how to construct good-working face masks at home, we noticed that having a basic understanding of the whole context of the pandemic and the virus in particular allowed us to make better decisions to keep ourselves and our families safe. We believe everybody who is trying to minimize the risk for an infection, will also be interested and benefit from such information.

We, therefore, set out to write a guide on making do-it-yourself face masks supplemented with an overview on the pandemic's origin and economic impact to all of us. With none of us ever having used a sewing machine before it was important for us to make these masks as effective as possible, while still easy to assemble. We therefore developed a mask design for any level of craft skills and material available: Perhaps you might be an amazing seamstress with a sewing machine handy. Great! You may want to use our advanced sewed face mask patterns to start your own line of designer face masks. But if you're like many of us—no sewing machine and/or no time or money to invest in one—then you might find the simple folded mask worth your while.

While we were researching and writing this book, we became more and more aware that in order to get the coronavirus outbreak under control, it is critical for everyone to better understand the virus, how to protect against it, and why wearing face masks can play such an essential role in this. We even want to make wearing face masks the new social norm, at least until the virus is gone.

Following this vision, the book is structured in three parts. Part one provides a general overview of what a virus is—more specifically, the novel coronavirus, how it spreads, and what measures could offer some sort of protection for yourself and your loved ones against it. Furthermore, we will uncover how face masks work, the different models available, and how to handle them. This part might be slightly lengthy for some readers. While this depth was required to explain the attributes of a face mask and develop our designs, it is meant as an introduction only and is not a prerequisite for making the face mask. The second part encompasses the main body of the book and will reveal in detail how to make different types of homemade face masks, including sewing patterns and step-by-step instructions. We understand that not all readers have access to or know how to use a professional sewing machine (again, we're right there with you), hence, we provide options to make your face mask with or without a sewing machine. We will also provide you with different size options. The third chapter gives a high-level overview of further protection measures you and your family or loved ones can take, such as disinfection of mail and groceries.

We want to note here that there is still debate over the effectiveness of wearing do-it-yourself face masks. Some tests, for example the ones performed by Dr. Segal at the Wake Forest Institute for Regenerative Medicine in Winston-Salem, N.C., conclude that these masks provide some level of protection. However, Dr. Segal also notes that "[...] homemade masks that used flimsier fabric tested as low as 1 percent filtration."[14] Therefore, the mask design, its material and the way it is used is very important. Further research is required on this topic before a conclusion can be drawn. We, therefore, encourage researchers, designers, tailors, inventors, and anyone else with creative ideas to help find better solutions and contribute to the debate. Researchers need to focus their effort on designing the optimal face mask that offers good protection at an affordable price and is reusable. If you have any ideas on how to improve our face mask designs or suggestions on the materials used, please contact us at <u>contact@Ceratul.com</u>.

Finally, we encourage everyone to make their own masks following our instructions and would be happy if any news coverage of our material helps spread the word. If you want to cover our material in an article or blog, or you would just like to share your experience or pictures of your own masks with us, then please also contact us at <u>contact@Ceratul.com</u>.

While we usually do not like showing ourselves and especially our families online, we are making an exception for this book with the hope that this helps to encourage some of you to wear face masks yourself and thus help making face mask the new social norm.

The Schwientek Family
California, United States

The von Butler Family
Bavaria, Germany

 It is important to provide some additional warning to all of you here before we continue.

Firstly, wearing a face mask, especially a do-it-yourself one, will **not** provide full protection against a virus. With all instructions we provide here, there will always be a risk of getting infected. To make matters worse, fidgeting with your mask could introduce germs to your face. Another big worry is that wearing a mask might make you start believing that you are protected more than you actually are. Sometimes, when people believe they are safe, they take an inappropriate level of risks, such as stopping and neglecting good hygiene or social distancing practices. We, therefore, urge you to never feel too safe and to only use a face mask as an additional measure to the measures provided by your local health authorities or your medical professional practitioner.

Secondly, the quality of do-it-yourself face masks greatly depends on the mask design, its material, its build process, and the way it is used.

Thirdly, we want to reiterate that none of the authors are authorized or qualified to provide medical or professional advice. We urge you to be careful and recommend you review any guidelines given here with your doctor or local health authority.

Overview of the virus and face masks

Nomenclature and origin of the virus

The media is full of news reporting on new coronavirus cases and COVID-19 statistics, but what exactly do these names mean and where do they originate? The first thing to understand is that there is a differentiation between the name of the disease and the name of the virus that is causing it. On February 11th of 2020, the World Health Organization (WHO) officially named the disease "coronavirus disease 2019" ("COVID-19" for short) which is characterized by symptoms of respiratory infections. This is distinct from the virus, which was named "severe acute respiratory syndrome coronavirus 2" ("SARS-CoV-2" for short). This name was chosen due to the genetic similarity to the coronavirus that caused the 2003 SARS outbreak.[15] SARS-CoV-2 is just one of a large family of coronaviruses, which are named for their crown-like ("coronam" is latin for "crown") appearance.

With clarity on the nomenclature, let's also talk briefly about what a virus is in the first place. The illustration on the right shows a single SARS-CoV-2 virion. Put simply, viruses are tiny envelopes (shown in gray) that contain

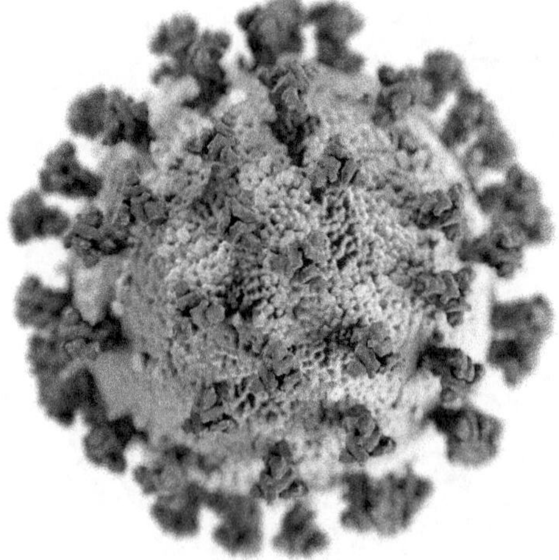

Ultrastructural morphology exhibited by coronaviruses. Parts are artificially colored: envelop (gray); Spike proteins (red). Virus diameter: 60-140nm.

Image by CDC on Unsplash, (https://unsplash.com/photos/k0KRNtqcjfw)

the blueprints for their own replication. The blueprint of SARS-CoV-2 comes in the form of an almost 30,000 nucleotide long sequence. Each nucleotide represents a piece of information that is collectively referred to ribonucleic acid (RNA). RNA is a derivative of deoxyribonucleic acid (DNA), which is how humans and even bacteria store their blueprints. Unlike bacteria however, viruses cannot replicate autonomously but instead rely on hijacking host cells for their replication. While there are many kinds of viruses that differ in shape and size as well as the way they inject their replication instructions into the host cell, SARS-CoV-2 accomplishes it through specialized "Spike" proteins (shown in red). These proteins cover the surface of the envelope and can efficiently attach to human cell receptors. Once attached to a cell, the virus envelope merges with the cell membrane and releases the blueprint for its own replication into the now infected cell. The host cell is then forced to use its own molecular machinery to read the virus' blueprint and begins to rapidly produce new virus parts that are subsequently assembled into fully functioning viruses. Once the host cell's resources are exhausted it dies and releases millions of new viruses into the environment, ready to infect cells in neighboring tissues.[16] This snow-ball effect continues unnoticed in the body of an infected person for several days - and in some cases without ever developing any symptoms at all. However, most people will begin to experience mild to moderate symptoms around 5 days after the infection (but this incubation period can vary between 2–14 days[17]). The symptoms often include dry cough, tiredness, and fever, which is a reaction of the body's immune system to the presence of the virus. After the detection of the virus by the immune system, the body begins production of highly specialized proteins, called antibodies. These antibodies are custom designed to attach to the virus, which renders it harmless and signals specialized immune cells to destroy it. Even long after all viruses are eradicated from the body and the individual has recovered, the immune system keeps copies of the antibodies against the specific virus. This generally gives recovered individuals immunity against future re-infections with the virus because new viruses will right away be bound by the antibodies and eliminated.

How the virus spreads

From the time of contracting the virus until the body's immune system has completely cleared the virus, an infected individual is considered a vector of COVID-19 (able to spread the disease). Even after a perceived recovery, however, the virus can still be in your body and linger for days on items and surfaces from which others can still contract the disease. It is therefore critical to follow the CDC's guidelines for how to discontinue home isolation[18] if you have been infected. Furthermore, proper disinfection of all surfaces and items you were in contact with should be carried out (see Disinfection of the virus). The primary established modes of transmission are:

- **Droplet**: The virus disseminates from the body when an infected person coughs, sneezes, or spits out. The resulting micro droplets may be loaded with viruses and can cause direct infection by entering the eyes, nose, mouth, or lungs through inhalation. Moreover, the droplets can fall onto clothes, body parts, and other items from which a contact transmission may occur. Droplet transmission is most likely when people are in close contact (within 3 feet / 1 meter). It is therefore important to keep a minimum of 6 feet (2 meters) distance

- **Contact**: Without following strict guidelines, an infected person can contaminate everything in his or her proximity. To prevent this, almost all local authorities have by now issued "stay at home" and "self-isolation" orders. However, even if everyone would comply with these orders (which is sadly not the case), those infected and in their incubation period may have already spread the virus without experiencing symptoms or being aware they are carrying the disease. In other words, they are asymptomatic. During essential errands, such as shopping for groceries, those who are infected may come in contact with shared items, such as shopping cards, keypads, door handles, gas pumps, etc. and not knowingly contaminate these surfaces. Hence, frequently touched surfaces and items are particularly prone for contamination when accessible to the public. Once the virus is on the hands of a healthy person, it may just take a rubbing of the eye or other touch to the face to contract the disease through contact transmission. It is therefore essential to frequently wash your hands and avoid touching your face. Wearing disposable gloves and a face mask in public as well as disinfecting frequently touched surfaces regularly are equally important.

- **Airborne**: There is growing evidence that the virus may also be transmitted through the air (e.g., by simply talking with an infected person even at a distance).[19] The difference compared to droplet transmission is that the exhaled droplets are much smaller and hence do not sink to the floor so quickly. Instead, they remain airborne for longer periods and can travel farther distances.

Why and when you should wear a face mask

We will go into more detail on face masks in a later chapter, but it is important to understand why and when to wear the proper face mask. There are two common types of commercially available face masks:

- **Surgical masks:** These simple masks are designed to protect patients and healthcare providers from infecting each other with potential germs originating in the respiratory system. While the effectiveness of these masks is being debated, it is generally accepted practice during the coronavirus outbreak for healthcare workers and other exposed workers to wear them for protection.
- **Respirators (e.g. N95):** These more sophisticated masks are designed to protect the wearer from germs and particulates of certain sizes in the environment. They filter the air prior to inhalation and catch germs on the outside. They provide adequate protection from contracting the virus through the respiratory system.

The US and other countries have recently changed course on guidelines of wearing face masks in public in that they now encourage everyone to wear them. This change is based on new research that suggests that the relatively high number of asymptomatic infected (including infected people during their incubation period) may pose a greater risk of spreading the disease than was initially known. The rationale by the CDC is therefore to have everybody wear masks for the primary purpose of decreasing the spread of the virus through droplet transmission by asymptomatic infected.[20] This is important to know as it determines what kind of face mask you should buy or build. That is, the general population should wear surgical masks or rather self-made equivalents to not compete with healthcare workers for personal protective equipment (PPE) who are at much higher risk of getting infected.

A recent Chinese study of coronavirus cases found that "undocumented infections were the infection source of 79% of documented cases", thus arguing that those cases with none or mild symptoms are the major reason for the wide spread of the disease.

Li et al.[20]

Depending on the materials chosen, self-made face masks can also add some protection against the virus' droplets. Self-made masks can therefore offer a certain level of protection when built, fit, and worn correctly. It should be noted that respirators and other professional masks generally offer higher protection than self-made masks. However, these masks are in dire need in hospital and first responder settings and should be donated to those institutions to better protect healthcare workers.

Where does the virus come from?

The novel SARS-CoV-2 coronavirus first emerged in December 2019 in the Chinese city of Wuhan, the capital of the Hubei province and the most populated city in central China with more than 10 million inhabitants. About two-thirds of the first forty-one COVID-19 cases were linked to the Huanan Seafood Wholesale Market in Wuhan, which caters to a growing Chinese consumer group that sees eating exotic foods as a status symbol. Besides seafood, around 120 different wildlife animals were regularly sold there and many of the early infected were wildlife traders working at the market. After the outbreak was recognized by the Chinese Center for Disease Control & Prevention, it was closed, and 585 samples were taken of which 33 tested positive for the virus. While the market clearly seemed to be a hot spot for the early transmission of the virus, it does not fully answer the question of the origin of the virus as multiple infected (including the very first case ever reported) never set foot on the market and no other connection could be identified.

On a genetic level, the coronavirus that is most closely related to SARS-CoV-2 was previously isolated from bats (species *Rhinolophus affinis*) and shares about 96% of its overall blueprint.[21] The closest matching Spike protein however, is found in a coronavirus that infects the malayan pangolins (species *Manis javanica*).[22] Both types of animals are considered exotic foods and sought after for their purported medicinal virtues. However, there has been no conclusive evidence that these animals were sold at the market. Furthermore, the genetic similarities are not close enough to make SARS-CoV-2 a likely direct progeny of either virus. Instead, it is more likely that a yet-to-be-identified intermediate host exists that carries the parent of SARS-CoV-2. This rationale follows the findings from previous viral outbreaks, such as the 2002 SARS and the 2012 Middle East Respiratory Syndrome (MERS) outbreaks, in which civets and camels, respectively were identified as intermediate hosts that were the missing link between bats and humans.

While viruses are usually specific to one host, prolonged exposure of humans to animals carrying viruses increases the chance of infection with spontaneously mutated versions of the virus that are able to infect humans. These cross-species infections may initially be asymptomatic and can remain undetected for prolonged periods of time. This gives the virus time to evolve and adapt to its new human host through mutation and natural selection until a specific set of mutations in its blueprint causes it to evolve into the highly infectious and sometimes lethal version that is currently spreading across the globe.[23]

On the other hand, it cannot be excluded that the virus was not directly transmitted from bats as in the case of MERS, where at least one bat was found carrying the exact virus that was also isolated from humans.[24] This is further supported by the fact that bats are known to be rich reservoirs of viruses, most of which are yet to be discovered and studied.[23]

Other, less likely theories are sometimes portrait in the media that involve the Wuhan Institute of Virology or the Wuhan Center for Disease Control & Prevention. Both research institutes study bats and the coronaviruses they carry and are located nine miles and less than one mile away from the Huanan market, respectively. However, it is highly unlikely that the virus is man-made or was purposefully created in one of these labs.[23]

In summary, while it is currently not known where the exact origin of the virus lies, it is most likely of natural origin and was transmitted to humans from wildlife in a similar manner as in previous viral outbreaks.

Why is the virus so dangerous?

Many factors play into the severity and death toll of a viral outbreak. Firstly, a coronavirus pandemic is a relatively rare event. Unlike the annual flu for example, our bodies have not seen a similar coronavirus before and consequently have no residual immunity against it. This is the same reason why there are no vaccinations and no specific medication available.[25] What's more, the hospitalization rate is about ten times higher for COVID-19 than for the flu, overwhelming the healthcare systems in many hotspot regions around the globe.[26] On top of that, about 5% of COVID-19 patients develop severe pneumonia and need artificial breathing assistance with a mechanical ventilator (breathing machine). Pneumonia is an infection of the lungs in which the air sacs swell due to inflammation, making it hard to breath and take up sufficient oxygen. In these cases, ventilators, in combination with oxygen therapy, can prevent death through suffocation. However, ventilators do nothing to curb the disease, they merely give the body's immune system more time to overcome the infection. While ventilators save lives, the survival rate of patients who are on ventilators is still low.

The shortage of ventilators often portrayed in the media is in part due to these machines being quite expensive ($25,000–$50,000) and them not being required in large numbers before the epidemic hit. Consequently, hospitals do not stockpile them and the manufacturing capacity for these quite complex machines is low and slow to ramp up to the large sudden demand (e.g. 40,000 ventilators for New York alone[27]). Furthermore, medical personnel need to go through specific training to be able to properly operate them.

The fatality rate of COVID-19 is currently a highly debated topic and exact numbers are very difficult to obtain. This is due to differences in how causes of death are reported. For example, a deceased individual could be reported as having died from pneumonia, from COVID-19, or another underlying health issue. That is if the person passed away in a hospital and got tested—not everybody is. What is clear, however, is that the elderly and those with underlying health problems, such as diabetes, severe obesity, moderate to severe asthma, chronic lung disease and immunocompromised, among others, are at higher risk for getting severely ill when infected.[28] It is this risk group in which the vast majority of COVID-19 related deaths occur. While there are certainly exceptions, one should keep in mind that hardly any corona-victim is subjected to an autopsy, which could reveal previously unknown health issues and perhaps better explain these unexpected cases in younger and seemingly healthy people. However, all the young and healthy people still not following the advice from authorities as they do not feel at risk should remember that with the shortage in hospital beds and health providers due to the coronavirus, they are at risk even for completely unrelated emergencies, such as a car accident. Therefore, keeping the outbreak under control must matter to everyone.

How to protect against COVID-19

In addition to wearing face masks, the key measures recommended by experts, for which amongst those include WHO and CDC specialists, are[8]:

- **Maintain social distancing**
  Maintain at least 3 feet (1 meter) of distance between yourself and anyone else; Ideally, extend the distance to 6 feet (2 meters).
- **Wash your hands frequently**
  Cleaning your hands frequently and thoroughly with soap and water or with an alcohol-based hand rub. Soap and high-percentage alcohol (>=60%) inactivates the virus.
- **Practice respiratory hygiene**
  Ensure you cover your mouth and nose with the inside of your bent elbow or a tissue when coughing or sneezing. If a tissue is used, dispose of it immediately and wash hands.

- **Avoid touching eyes, nose and mouth**
  Your hands get contaminated with the virus quickly through touching infected people or surfaces. Once contaminated, touching your eyes, nose or mouth can transfer the virus and promote an infection.
- **If you are symptomatic, i.e. you have fever, dry cough or difficulty breathing, you need to seek medical advice immediately**
  To protect yourself and others, stay at home if you feel unwell. Should you develop symptoms typical of the coronavirus, seek medical advice immediately. Instead of rushing to the hospital, it is best to call your doctor or your local health authority in advance to seek further appropriate instructions. Always call 911 in an emergency situation.
- **Keep yourself informed and up to date on the most recent coronavirus developments and follow the advice given by your local health authority**
  Staying informed and up to date on the most recent coronavirus developments is key. This will allow you to know the latest recommendations to protect yourself and your loved ones, as well as better understand the outbreak situation in your local area. Your local health authority, as well as the national health authority, will issue advice and rules on the coronavirus.

How face mask help protect against viruses

The previous sections helped to understand what the virus is and especially, how it spreads, which is key to you being able to protect yourself and your family. Especially the information around the size of the virus is crucial, when it comes to assessing the level of protection various purchased or homemade face masks can provide.

In this section, we will provide an overview of how face masks actually work and help to protect against viruses, compare different types of face masks, explain the lifetime of face masks, as well as outline the most recent expert guidelines on face masks. Furthermore, we will provide some additional justification on why buying medical-grade face masks is not a sustainable option for the majority of people.

How face masks work and why you should wear them

Face masks come in many forms, and we will explain the most common models in the next section. In general, most face masks, such as the well-known (and now short in supply) surgical face mask, are loose-fitting, disposable devices that act as a physical barrier between the wearer and their surrounding environment. These face masks are intended to block large-particle droplets and sprays from the wearer's nose and mouth that can potentially infect their direct surroundings. To a lesser extent, they also protect the wearer from coming into contact with droplets and sprays in their surroundings.

> **"Covid-19 moves like a silent assassin, with unwitting accomplices. Maybe you'll be one of them. The best way to ensure that you're not: wear a mask, and keep your distance from others. [...] almost any kind of simple cloth covering over your mouth, such as a home-made mask, or even a bandanna, can stop the assassin in its tracks."**
>
> ***Jeremy Howard, The Guardian*[29]**

Recent studies confirmed that merely breathing and speaking causes airborne virus particles from spreading and thus just avoiding being infected by someone sneezing or coughing is not enough.[30] Therefore, protection against droplet transmission is now more important than ever before. While most masks, including surgical face masks, are not designed to protect fully against inhalation of airborne viruses, such as the coronavirus, there is evidence that surgical masks filter out a portion of viruses.[30] A study from 2013 found that "Both [homemade and surgical] masks significantly reduced the number of microorganisms expelled by volunteers, although the surgical mask was 3 times more effective in blocking transmission than the homemade mask."[31] Summing up the evidence, many governments and institutions are now recommending that the best way to ensure that you are not getting others infected is to wear a mask, keep your distance from others and follow all other preventive measures. Therefore, both, surgical and homemade face masks provide some level of protection. While most research clearly shows that surgical masks are more effective than homemade masks, we need to note here that most of these studies assumed simple, non-improved homemade masks. Many homemade face masks analyzed in these studies neither used a filter, nor ensured improved fit through the usage of a nose piece and better design.

"The best homemade masks in his [Dr. Segal's] study were as good as surgical masks or slightly better, testing in the range of 70 to 79 percent filtration."

Tara Parker-Pope, New York Times[14]

We did, however, find two exceptions. One was from tests performed by Dr. Segal at the Wake Forest Institute for Regenerative Medicine in Winston-Salem, N.C., which reveal that "the best homemade masks in his [Dr. Segal's] study were as good as surgical masks or slightly better, testing in the range of 70 to 79 percent filtration. Homemade masks that used flimsier fabric tested as low as 1 percent filtration [though]."[14] The other involves a study carried out by Dr. Yang Wang, an assistant professor of environmental engineering at Missouri University of Science and Technology, who researched on the filter effectiveness of various materials. He found that "an allergy-reduction heating, ventilation, and air conditioning (HVAC) filter worked the best, capturing 89 percent of particles with one layer and 94 percent with two layers. A furnace filter captured 75 percent with two layers, but required six layers to achieve 95 percent."[14] Not bad at all compared to typical surgical face masks that have a filter efficiency ranging from 60 to 80 percent.

Studies of face masks came to the conclusion that the effectiveness of masks greatly depends on the filter material used, a good fit or seal over the nose and mouth, as well as how it is used. Therefore, we experimented with various designs and filter materials when we developed our face masks, as well as the recommendations for filter materials. We cannot conclude with certainty that this significantly improves the effectiveness of these masks as we lack the expertise and equipment to perform high quality testing at this point in time; however, based on the studies we reviewed, the improved design and filter material recommendations should raise the effectiveness of homemade masks.

We must keep these facts in mind when producing and wearing our homemade face masks, as the ultimate goal must be to have a good filter material and very close fit over nose and mouth.

Before we go on to explaining how to make your own masks, let us compare the most common types.

Difference between face mask and respirator models

With so much information on face masks and respirators floating around the internet, it can be challenging to understand your options. In the following, we will explain the key attributes driving the filter efficiency before taking a look at the different face mask types that are commercially available. As explained above, face masks and respirators collect particles through one or multiple physical mechanisms:

1. **The air filtration:**
   The air filtration efficiency is classified using the N-standard in the US and the P-classes in the EU. The standards indicate the % of airborne particles being filtered by the mask, e.g. a N95 mask filters at least 95% of airborne particles. Standard surgical masks have a simple filter layer, while the N95 filter class uses an additional charged filter material, which collects particles of smaller sizes due to its electrostatic attraction. In general, each type of filter has a certain particle size range that it can collect and, thus, filter out. The flow of air also impacts the ability of the filter efficiency. As flow increases, particles in the filter range are filtered out less efficiently.[32]

2. **Fit of the mask or respirator:**
   The fit of the mask or respirator measures the leakage around the facepiece, i.e. how much airflow is not going through the filter material. With loose-fitted surgical masks, the unfiltered airflow is fairly high compared to well fitted respirators.

Now let's compare the different types of face mask and respirator models:

Type	Description	Usage	COVID-19 use
Do-it-yourself mask	Can help protect wearers and their surroundings to a certain degree from airborne viruses, especially in terms of preventing a sick wearer from infecting others; however, fit and filter quality greatly vary depending on the design and material used	Reusable (when disinfected properly after each usage)	Recently being recommended by several government authorities for everyone to wear
Surgical mask	Can help protect wearers and their surroundings to a certain degree from airborne viruses; mainly used by healthcare workers so that they do not infect patients	Disposable mask for single usage	Mainly recommended for healthcare workers and other exposed people
N95 respirator	Commonly used by craftsmen, especially working with wood, as well as by medical staff. Filters at least 95% of airborne particles.	Disposable mask for single usage	Mainly recommended for healthcare workers and other exposed people
Powered air-purifying respirator	Used where protection against gases is required or where medical staff and researchers work with hazardous or dangerous material. They are usually made from a headgear, a powered fan, one or multiple filters and a power supply.	Reusable	No recommendation known to us
Self-contained breathing apparatus	Known to be worn by firefighters and divers; used to provide breathable air in an environment that would else not supply breathable air, for example under water or in case of heavy smoke in a fire.	Reusable	No recommendation known to us

Authorities across the globe now recommend wearing masks for the general public

With so much evidence at hand that supports wearing of face masks, it comes as no surprise that governments and health authorities around the world have changed their opinion on face masks and now recommend wearing them in the general public. Several EU countries, amongst others the Czech Republic, Poland and Slovakia, now require everyone to wear face masks, with Austria following the recommendation[33] and calls in Germany are growing for country-wide use of face masks. Some Asian countries, China, Hong Kong, Japan, South Korea, Thailand and Taiwan, to name the most prominent examples, "are urging everyone to wear a mask, and in some parts of China you could even be arrested and punished for not wearing one."[34]

Even the U.S. Surgeon General Dr. Jerome Adams, who famously twittered "Seriously people, STOP BUYING MASKS!"[35] at the onset of the pandemic outbreak in the US has revised his standing and now shows how to make homemade face masks in a video.[36]

Is it safe to reuse a face mask?

Every respirator and surgical mask, even the ones intended for reuse, have a limited lifetime after which the mask itself, or in the case of reusable masks—its filters, need(s) to be replaced. The exact lifetime of the respirators and masks depends on many factors, and you always need to follow the specifications provided by the manufacturer. The CDC has published recommendations on the lifetime of the N95 respirator devices and maximum reusage.[37] But these N95 respirator are from different material and provide a different level of protection. Most sources still recommend disposing surgical face masks after every use.[38]

Most experts still recommend disposing surgical face masks after every use.

There is no conclusive evidence on the lifetime of a homemade face mask, and it will greatly differ depending on the design, material used, personal usage and environment it is exposed to. However, certain designs of homemade masks can possibly be disinfected, either by washing with detergent or other means of disinfection—see chapter three for suggestions on disinfection of your face mask. Depending on the means of disinfection and design of the mask, this might allow for reuse. While conclusive evidence is yet to be provided, this might extend the lifetime of a homemade mask. It is generally recommended to dispose face masks of any making if they get contaminated with blood or bodily secretions from others, are damaged, or hard to breathe through.[37]

Regardless of the mask and its lifetime, you must closely follow the general recommendations on putting the mask on, wearing it, and taking it off, which we explain later when reviewing how to use your mask.

Why purchasing face masks is not a solution

While hardly anybody outside of Asia thought about wearing face masks until a few weeks ago, they have now become one of the most sought after products on the global market: The coronavirus has seen prices for masks surge by 2,000% in some countries[39] and spurred a "wild west" battle over supply that is dividing even NATO allies.[40] With the US and other authorities now recommending for the general public to wear face masks, demand is going to skyrocket and make it impossible for global production to keep up with demand. To make matters worse, many producing countries have banned the export of face masks,[41] completely undermining the global supply chain and spurring a global trade war over face masks. With demand skyrocketing and prices going up, scammers have taken advantage of this as an opportunity to make money from the desperate need of billions; Counterfeits of malfunctioning face masks are becoming more frequent, and even governments, as in the Spanish case of faulty coronavirus test kits shows,[42] are not able to protect themselves against scammers. How should consumers be able to find out what is a scam and what is real in such an environment? The ones to suffer are medical health workers and the general public, who can no longer protect themselves against a virus infection.

But even without these dramatic developments on the global face mask market, it is highly unlikely that global production could keep up with the demand. Over 50% of the world's 7.8 billion people are already in lock down today,[4] and many experts expect that up to 70% of the world's population will get infected by the coronavirus.[43]

Looking at these numbers, one can assume that all the world's 7.8 billion people should be recommended to wear some sort of face mask for protection. With at least a daily replacement of face masks and an estimated duration of the pandemic of at least 12 months,[44] we are looking at a demand of approximately two trillion eight hundred billion face masks over the next 12 months.

Cost of face masks for average family

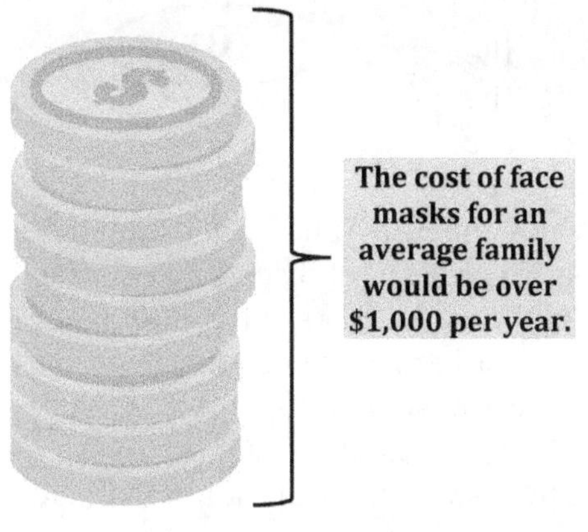

Source: Own estimates

We expect this to be a conservative estimate, given that it is generally recommended to replace face masks more frequently. Furthermore, demand will certainly stay very high, even after the pandemic.[45]

Even at the pre-pandemic prices of $0.2 per disposable surgical face masks, the total cost of face mask supply would be $570 billion and at current prices of over $1 per face mask, we could be looking at as much as $3 trillion.[46] The cost of face masks for an average family would be over $1,000 per year; and this is assuming a reuse of face masks with an exchange rate of possibly only once per day.

Even if production volume could be ramped up to meet demand and families would carve out enough money to afford buying masks, the environmental impact would be devastating. Assuming a 0.1 cm thickness of surgical masks, the waste pile would be 2.8 million km high or 70x the circumference of the world. That would be an incredibly large pile of waste and with the demand of face masks remaining high even after the pandemic, this would become a massive drain on global resource availability and waste capacity.

Based on all of this evidence and expert opinions, the only viable option we see at this point in time, unless the situation changes, is to revert to reusable homemade masks for the global population, while keeping the filtering facepiece respirators and more protective surgical face masks reserved for healthcare workers. And while the CDC and other reputable sources have advised the need to reserve these medical-grade respirators and face masks for healthcare workers, we cannot ignore that there are many other front-line workers who need the same level of protection, such as grocery store (or similar food and produce) workers and delivery workers. We ultimately need to invest in research to find the optimal design and materials for homemade masks. The U-turn in recommendations from governments and both national and global institutions around the usage of cloth masks and homemade masks underlines this statement.

Waste pile of face masks would go around earth 70x

Source: Own estimates

Making your own face masks at home

In non-emergency situations one should always opt for professional factory-produced protective gear. However, as the current pandemic has shown and as explained above, there might be situations in which surgical masks or filtering facepiece respirators are not an option for multiple reasons:

1. Commercial protective masks are sold out and, if at all, can only be purchased at prices that are not sustainable for an average household.
2. Supply shortage requires rationing for medical and exposed cohorts only, leaving the general public with little to no protection and greater fear and anxiety.
3. Leaving the house to purchase masks might put you at higher risk.
4. Delivery times are too long for the urgent need.

 In such situations, you might need to use what is at your disposal to create the best possible protection for you and your loved ones using items you already have in your household or can purchase easily at a low cost and with low risk.

As mentioned before, none of the authors ever used a sewing machine, so it was important for us to develop mask designs that are effective, while still easy to make. We therefore heavily researched the coronavirus, its transmission, face masks in general and filter materials, as well as face mask designs to develop face masks that offer a reasonable level of filtration, while being low cost and easy to make. The level of protection of a face mask is mainly impacted by the filter used within the mask and the fit of the mask, which in turn is determined by the nose piece, size of the mask, and the earpieces. We therefore assessed four attributes:

1. **Filter material:** The effectiveness of the filter material used and its characteristics in terms of breathability

2. **Face mask design:** The effectiveness of preventing aerosol penetration of nose and mouth of various face mask designs
3. **Difficulty to "do it yourself":** The difficulty level of making various face mask designs with diverse materials yourself at home
4. **Availability and affordability of material:** The availability and affordability of the various materials required to make masks

Using these attributes, we looked at over 100 different combinations of face mask designs and filter materials to develop five homemade face mask recommendations.

The five designs we explain in this book in more detail are 1) the folded cloth mask, 2) the sewed mask without filter, 3) the sewed mask with filter, 4) the improved sewed mask without filter and 5) the improved sewed mask with filter.

Additional to these designs, we have developed an even more advanced face mask design. This design requires more sophisticated sewing skills and explaining it here in the required detail would make the lengths of this book get out of hand. We therefore limit the instructions for this advanced sewed face mask to providing you with the sewing patterns and a one-pager instruction in chapter *Sewing patterns, size chart and further designs.*

Below we provide a summary of the five masks and explain them in more detail in the following pages.

Type	Description	Material required	Tools required
Folded cloth mask **Difficulty**: Low	Simple folded mask made from a bandana, t-shirt or any sort of cloth. Only requires the piece of cloth and two elastic bands. Additionally, a wire can be used to add a nosepiece.	• Square cloth from high-quality cotton or a bandana • Rubber band, hair band or elastic sewing band • Paperclip, twist tie, or wire (optional)	• Scissors or utility knife • Measuring tape or ruler • Marker
Sewed mask with and without filter **Difficulty**: Low	Simple sewed mask made from high-quality cotton. Adds additional comfort and fit through an ear- and nosepiece. Requires basic sewing skills, as well as more material and tools than the folded cloth mask.	• Piece of cloth from quilted cotton or 100% cotton cloth • Elastic sewing band or elastic hair ties • Crafting or gardening wire • Filter material (optional)	• Scissors • Tape measure or ruler • Pencil • Pins and thread • Sewing machine or a sewing needle • Iron and desk (optional)
Improved sewed mask with and without filter **Difficulty**: Medium	Improved sewed mask that adds additional comfort through a design that better covers the nose and mouth. Requires intermediate sewing skills, as well as more material and tools than the folded cloth mask.	Same as above	Same as above

This is how our selection of sewed masks looks like—you can make one to fit any occasion and outfit.

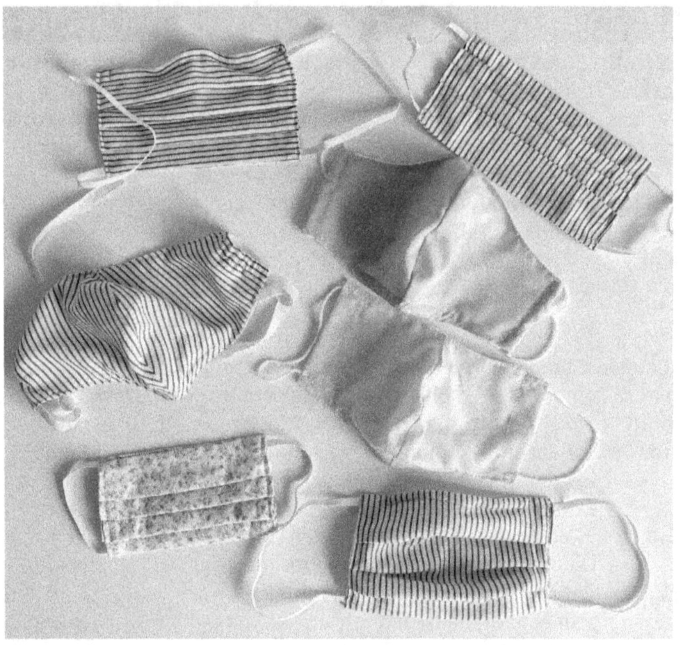

Please note: As we do not possess the required research tools or expertise to assess the effectiveness of these face mask designs or material ourselves, we cannot provide any guidance on their effectiveness and where stated, are only referring to others' research results in terms of filter effectiveness.

Key components of a face mask

Before we explain how to make a homemade face mask, we want to get into some more detail about the components a face mask is usually made from in order to understand them better. The key components of a face mask are:

1. **The cover material:** This is the main material of the mask, used to cover the filter and make the mask comfortable to wear. In some cases, as explained in the next sections, the cover material can also act as filter.

2. **The filter:** It is used to filter out particles and greatly impacts the effectiveness of face masks. In some cases, as explained in the next sections, the cover material can also act as filter.
3. **The nose piece:** Some masks come with a special nose piece, that allows the mask to better cover the nose and therefore further reduce in- and outflow of particles.
4. **The earpiece:** This is used to attach the mask to the wearer's head, allowing it to sit firmly over nose and mouth and thus reduce in- and outflow of particles.

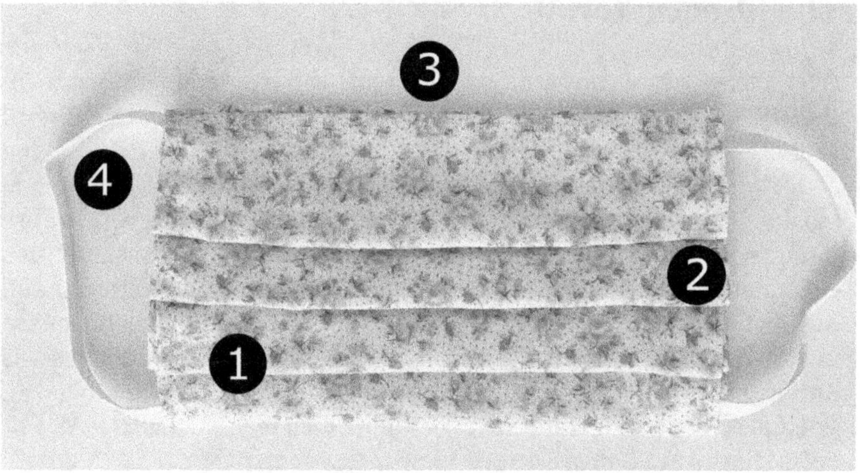

The following section will explain each of these components in some more detail. There are a few general tips for the cover and filter material, you need to keep in mind:

- To test the breathability of your material, layer two sheets of the material on top of each other, put them over your mouth and nose and breath. You only got the right material if breathing is easy and feels natural.
- While a very rough estimate, you can test the filter efficiency of your material by holding it up against a light and seeing how much light comes through. If a lot of light comes through, then your material is not thick enough and filtering will be inefficient.
- We are explaining various methods for disinfecting your mask in the disinfection chapter. If you want to use

boiling as method, then you need to use boil-proof cotton for the cover and filter material and pre-boil your cover and filter material before cutting it into the right size and starting to sew or preparing your mask. That is because boiling the mask later will shrink the fabrics. Therefore, use a larger piece of your cover material than required for sewing, boil it 3–4 times and dry it after each boiling process. Only cut the material into the right size after this process to avoid shrinking later on.

The filter material

Over the recent weeks, and especially as the pandemic outbreak hit the US, several researchers have studied the filter effectiveness of various household materials. We applaud these researchers for taking action and helping the public make better choices for their homemade masks. With experts expecting the pandemic to last several more months, if not years, we hope for researchers to continue this excellent work and to further study the most effective material and design for face masks. When trying to find the best filter material, we need to remember that not only the filtration effectiveness is important, but also the breathability and safety needs to be looked at. Vacuum cleaner bags and HEPA (High-Efficiency Particulate Air) or HVAC filters are being recommended in some YouTube videos and self-help blogs; however, researchers and filter producers warn that it might be dangerous to use these filters.[47,48] That is because some of these filters contain microscopic glass fibers that when released and inhaled can be harmful. Therefore, please follow the

instructions provided by the manufacturer if you plan to use any such filters. We generally recommend only using materials that are either used for wearing on the skin, such as cotton, safe for food production, or are recommended by the manufacturer for usage in face masks.

Overall, we assessed a number of materials for their filter effectiveness and their breathability as well as safe use. To compile these recommendations, we did our own tests with household materials we had available and compared sources from Cambridge University Press[31], The New York Times[14] and SmartAir[49]. Especially the Cambridge University Press study, called "Testing the Efficacy of Homemade Masks: Would They Protect in an Influenza Pandemic?", provides extremely helpful insights. This study performed experiments on various household materials and their ability to filter particles, compared against surgical masks. The study ensured that both, the average human aerosol flow, the particle size and the fitting of masks was tested under meaningful conditions. The study used an aerosol flow at 30 L/min, which is about the right flow to capture average human air flow across different situations. It "is about 3 to 6 times per minute the ventilation of a human at rest or doing light work, but is less than 0.1 the flow of an average cough."[31] The fit of the masks was tested across a number of different exercises, ranging from normal breathing over moving up and down to talking and light exercise. Testing against the right size of particles is very important, but equally difficult. While coronavirus itself is only around 0.1 microns, "it floats around in a wide range of sizes, from around 0.2 to several hundred microns, because people shed the virus in respiratory fluid droplets that also contain lots of salts and proteins and other things."[14] The studies we compared analyzed particles in the range of 0.02, 0.3 and 1 microns.

Based on the findings of these studies and our own tests, we recommend the usage of two layers of a heavyweight "quilter's cotton" or, if that is not available, two layers of a 100% cotton or cotton mix material, e.g. from a t-shirt or a pillowcase.

We recommend the usage of two layers of a heavyweight "quilter's cotton", or if that is not available two layers of a 100% cotton or cotton mix material, e.g. from a t-shirt or a pillowcase.

Quilted cotton   *100% cotton or cotton mix*   *Pillowcase*

We arrived at these recommendations by comparing the filter effectiveness and breathability, as well as safety, of various household material. The graph below shows how effective various material is in filtering particles of a size of 0.02 and 0.3 microns. Where significant or relevant improvements of filter efficiency was achieved by increasing the number of layers, we used an increased layer count for the graphic.

Filter effectiveness of 0.02 and 0.3 micron particle sizes

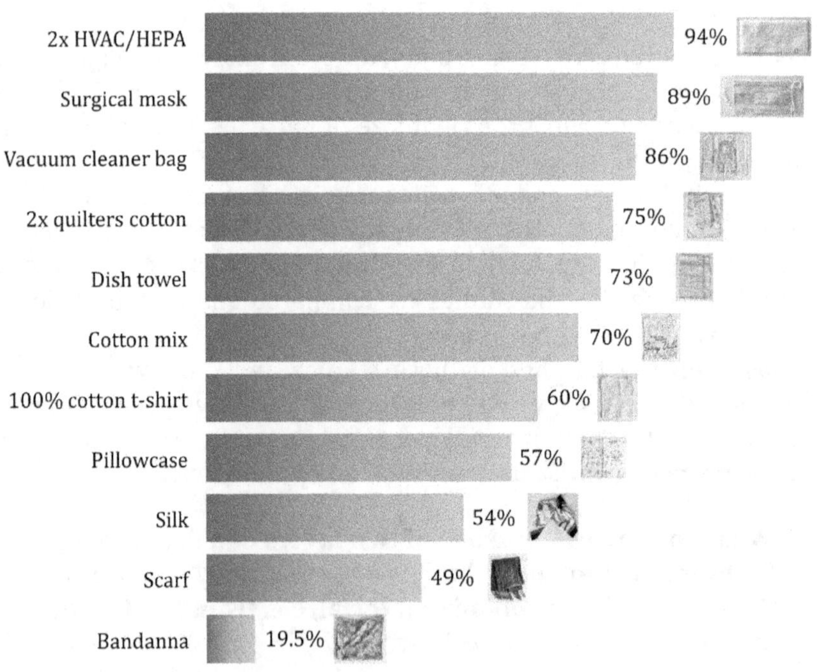

The second key factor is the breathability and safety of the materials. The Cambridge study tested this by comparing the pressure drop across fabrics. For easier comparability, we have set the most breathable material, the pillowcase, at 100% breathability and compared all other material relative to it. The tests show that four materials, the pillowcase, 100% cotton t-shirt, silk and quilter's cotton have a higher breathability than a surgical mask. In contrast, all other materials are more difficult to breathe through, with dish towels and vacuum cleaners being the hardest to breathe through. Both vacuum cleaners and HEPA/HVAC filters of some brands contain microfibers, and we do not recommend using them, unless specifically approved by the manufacturer.

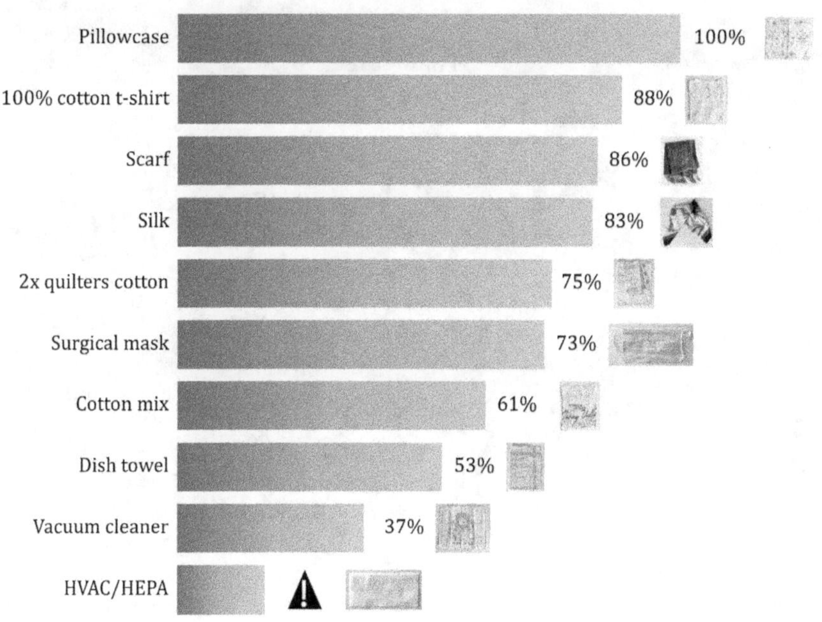

Breathability of household materials
Relative to the breathability o pillowcases

Source: Cambridge University Press, The New York Times, SmartAir and own estimates

Assessing the filter effectiveness and the breathability together, we see that two layers of a heavyweight "quilter's cotton", or if that is not available two layers of a 100% cotton or cotton mix material, e.g. from a t-shirt or a pillowcase should be the recommended materials for use in homemade face masks. This comes in handy as higher-grade commercial materials, such as surgical mask material, as well as the potentially harmful HEPA/HVAC filters, that are recommended in many self-help blogs and YouTube videos, will become short in supply very quickly if used for mainstream masks.

A benefit of using the recommended materials for the face mask is that this means no special filter is required. The cloth from which you make the mask already does the filtering, so it is not required to have a special filter pockets in your design. We will still show you a design with a filter pocket, you can use this in case you have filter material form a surgical mask or an HEPA/HVAC or vacuum cleaner bag approved for such usage.

Finding the optimal material for face mask filters

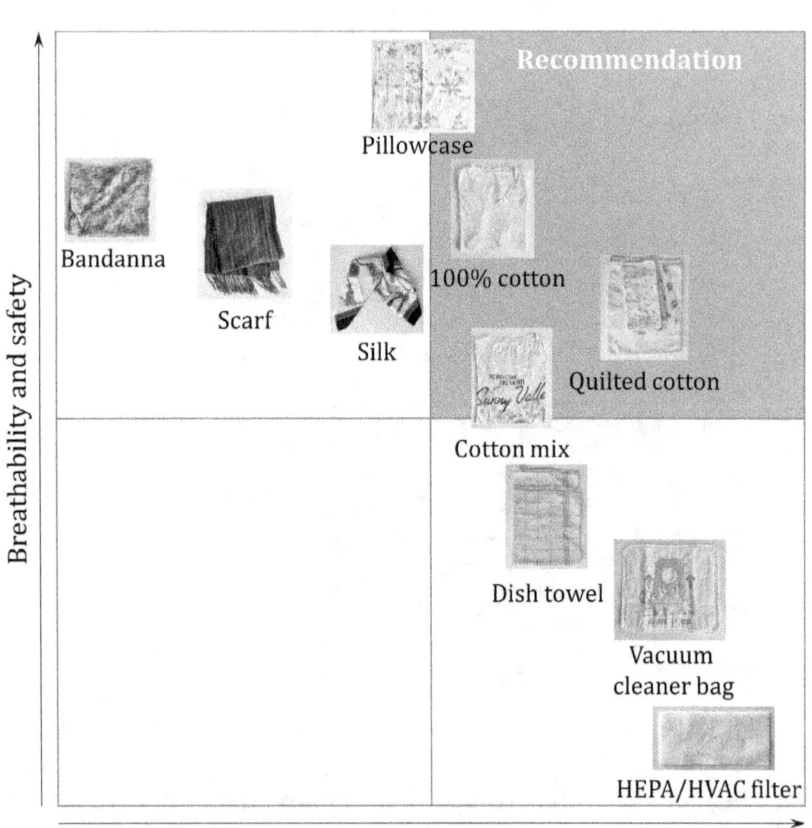

The cover materials

Next to the filter material, the cover material is important for a homemade face mask. The cover material needs to be safe to wear, breathable, and, of course, comfortable to wear. We recommend using the same material as for the filter, quilter's cotton or 100% mixed cotton from t-shirts or pillowcases. This makes the production process a lot easier and means you need less material. You can of course also use material such as quilted cotton or 100% cotton t-shirts for the filter layers only and then have a more appealing material, such as silk, as your cover material. However, please remember to choose a material that has good breathability and is safe.

Quilted cotton

100% cotton or cotton mix

Pillowcase

The earpiece

Both, the earpiece and nosepiece are key to ensure a proper fit of the face mask, and therefore improved protection. Some studies have noted that the need to tie some homemade masks at the back, rather than using elastic bands that fit them, greatly impacts the variability of the unfiltered air inflow. We therefore recommend using elastic sewing bands. If not available, you can also use elastic hair bands. Regular medium-width rubber bands will work as well, albeit they tend to pull on the hair around the ear making them a bit painful to put on and take off.

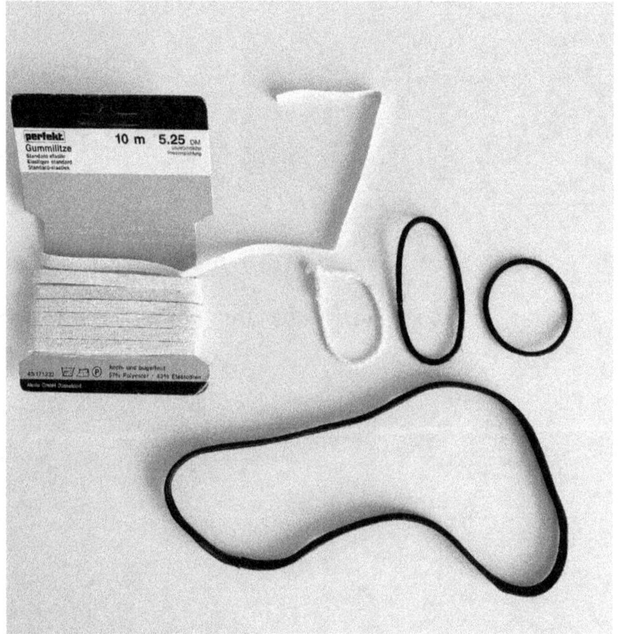

The nosepiece

There is a lot of debate around the nosepiece for homemade face masks; however, our tests and various studies show that using some sort of nosepiece helps to ensure that the mask better covers the face and therefore prevents unfiltered air inflow. You can use some sort of solid-core wire (18–20 gauge is ideal) or metal strip, for example a paper clip, crafting wire, or a binding strip, to fit the nosepiece.

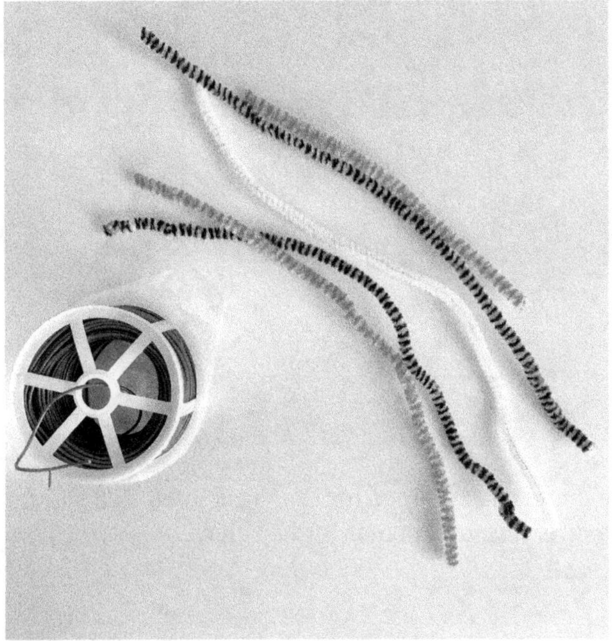

However, this does make the sewing process more difficult and requires some more advanced sewing skills.

Material for assembling the masks

Depending on the mask type, you will need:

- For the folded cloth mask, you need only the material for the mask and no special equipment

- The sewed and improved sewed face mask require either a sewing needle and thread or ideally a sewing machine

This is how our table looked like when we prepared for the mask assembly.

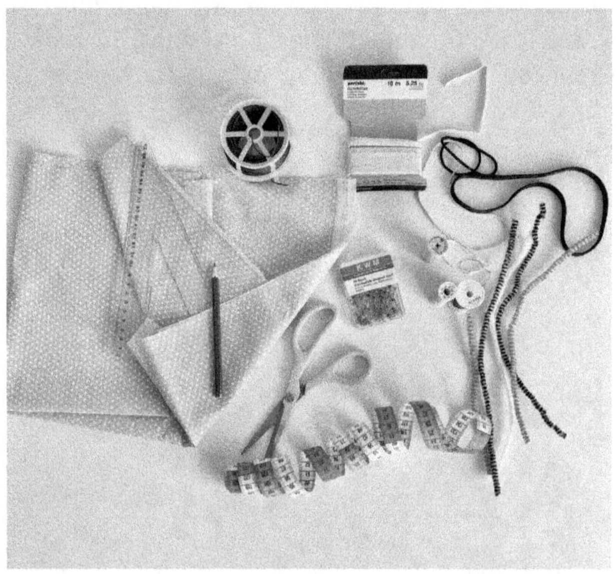

Next to the material explained for the mask itself, you should also have a tape measure, scissors, pencil, and a ruler.

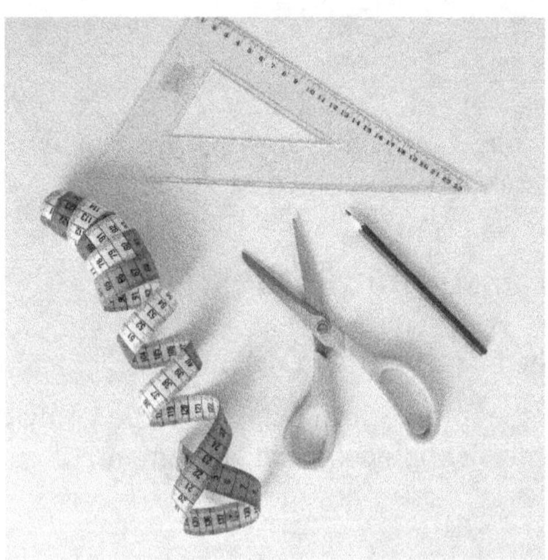

How to use your mask

Before diving into the making of masks, we will briefly cover the key steps of how to handle them properly. To start with, always wash your hands or apply an alcohol-based hand sanitizer before touching a clean mask. Likewise, disinfect your hands after handling a used and potentially contaminated mask.[50]

Putting it on

Putting it on should be straight forward when using elastic earpieces. Some masks come with simple straps that are more difficult to tie down on your own. If you can, ask a family member to assist you. Ensure there are no gaps between your face and the mask.

Fitting it

Please refer to the picture below for more details on how to fit your mask.

- The best materials and mask designs don't help if the air you breathe is not forced through the filter material. This most commonly happens through gaps that are formed between the nose and cheek (see points 2 and 3 in the picture below). Press the fabric into this gap to reduce unfiltered airflow. A simple pinch along the bridge of the nose can help ensure this area is sealed (see point 2 in the picture below). Breathe out several times while cupping your hands around the outer edges of the mask to detect any significant leaks.
- Another common culprit for improper seals are beards! So gentlemen, it is time to cut that facial hair back (to a short mustache if you have to keep some hair).
- The earpiece is another important part to optimize. It should push the mask snug to your face (see point 1 in the picture below). Adjust the size of the elastic band if you feel the mask is too loose by either tying a small part off, using a knot strapping it around the back of your head using, for example, a paper clip or safety pin (see

point 5 in the picture below). When making your mask, try the earpieces on before attaching them, so that you chose the right size.

- Also ensure that you are wearing the right mask size for your face. The mask should comfortably cover all of your nose, mouth and chin without obstructing your view. If you notice the folds in the fabric towards the ears, your mask may be too large for your face.

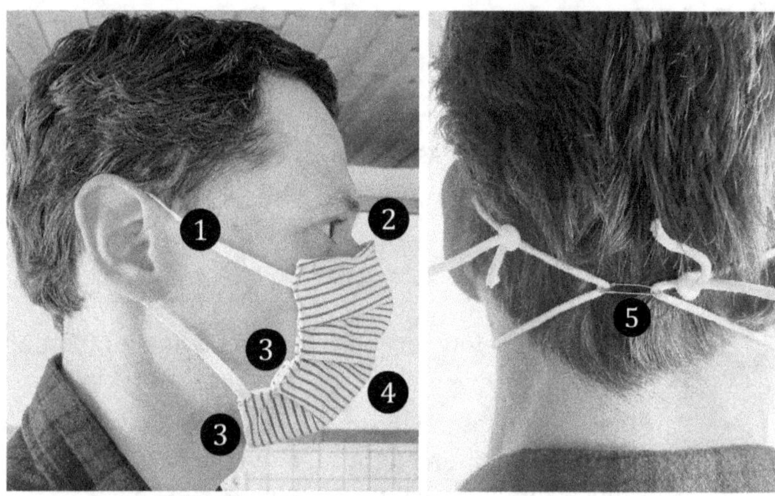

Well fitted mask   *Optional earpiece tie*

Wearing it

There is not too much to discuss here. Just be aware that exercising in your mask increases the airflow that is forced through the fabric and can reduce the filtering efficiency. Getting it wet, e.g. from walking in the rain, can also have undesirable consequences. Also, try to avoid sneezing and coughing into the mask or at least suppress the intensity as you will likely still force droplets out of the mask that could harm others if you happen to be an asymptomatic infected.[51] Lastly, avoid touching the mask while wearing it. It could transfer the virus to your hands. Use hand sanitizer or wash your hands with soap and water for at least 20 seconds if you had to touch it.

Taking it off

Remove the mask by taking off the earpieces. Be careful not to touch your face. Do not touch the fabric of the mask as it could be contaminated. If you are using single-use masks, dispose of them immediately into a closed bin, preferentially outside your home. For reusable home-made masks, collect used masks in an airtight container, such as a Ziplock bag, or gently place it directly into the washing machine (see chapter Disinfection of the Virus for a full guide on how to properly re-use masks). Wash your hands with soap and water for at least 20 seconds after handling used masks of any kind. If you suspect you've touched your face or any part of your head upon taking off the used mask, consider washing your face or taking a shower using your usual facial and/or body cleansers.

Folded cloth mask

Out of the five face mask designs we explain in this book, this is definitely the simplest to make and requires no sewing whatsoever. It is quite similar to the one recommended by the US Surgeon General,[52] but features several improvements. Based on the evidence we showed in the filter material section, this mask's design uses multiple layers of cloth material that act as the filter. It can easily be upgraded with a basic nose piece to improve the fit around the bridge of the nose, although this is optional.

What you need

Consumables

- Filter material: Square cloth from quilted cotton or 100% cotton cloth approximately 20" x 20" (50 cm x 50 cm), alternatively you can use a dish towel or bandana, but the latter will reduce the filter effectiveness significantly.
- Earpiece: Rubber band, hair band or elastic sewing band
- Nosepiece: paperclip or 4–5" (10–13 cm) of wire (optional)

- To assemble the mask: Scissors to cut your cloth, a tape measure or ruler and a pencil

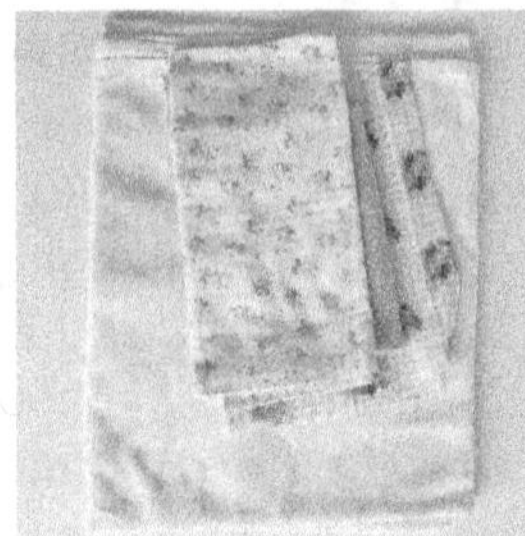

Quilted cotton

100% cotton or cotton mix

Pillowcase

Tools

- Scissors
- Measuring tape or ruler
- Marker
- Pliers (optional)

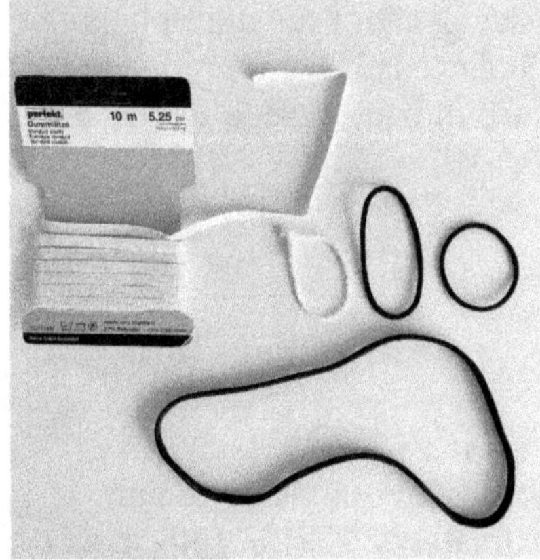

Elastic sewing band or elastic hair ties

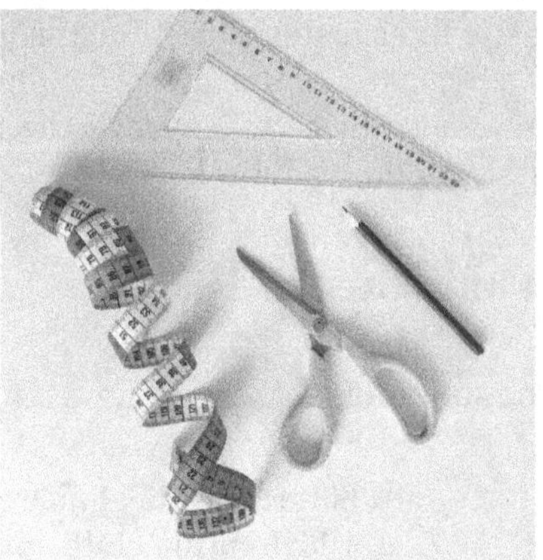

Tape measure, scissors, pencil and ruler

Preparation

Lay out your filter material flat on a table or the floor. Draw a square with a side length of approximately 18–20 inches (45–50 cm) using a measuring tape or ruler. Then using your scissors, cut out the square.

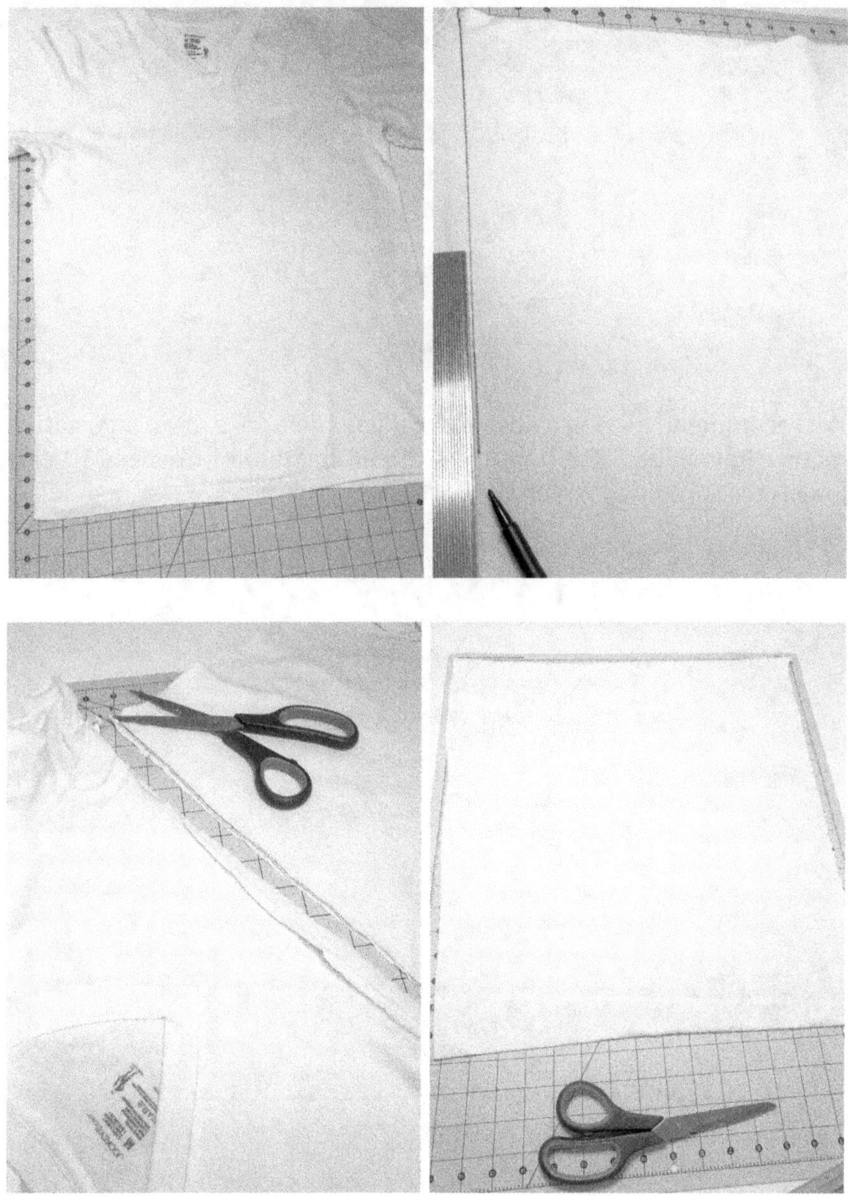

If you are using elastic sewing band, cut two strips to 6–8 inches (15–20 cm) in length and tie the ends of each together, forming two circles.

We recommend adding a nose piece if you have wire or an alternative material available. The final wire should be about 4 inches (10 cm) long (most unfolded paper clips are).

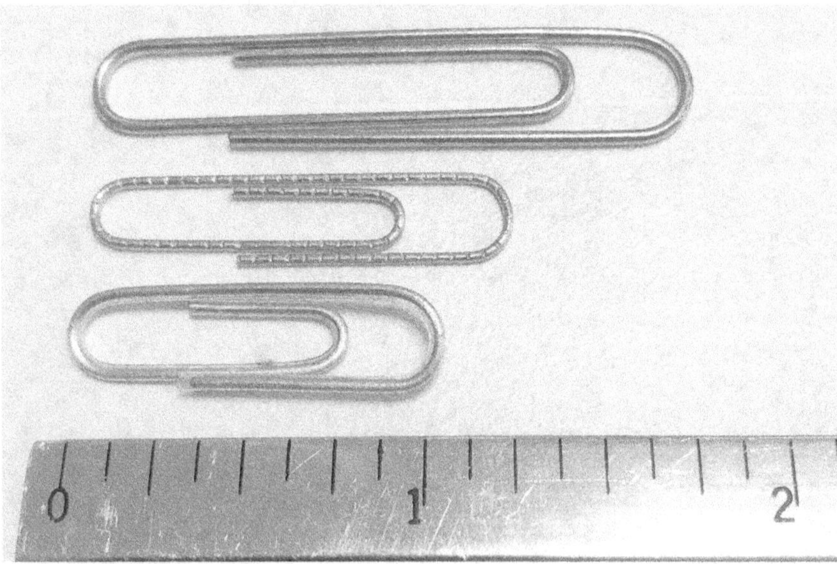

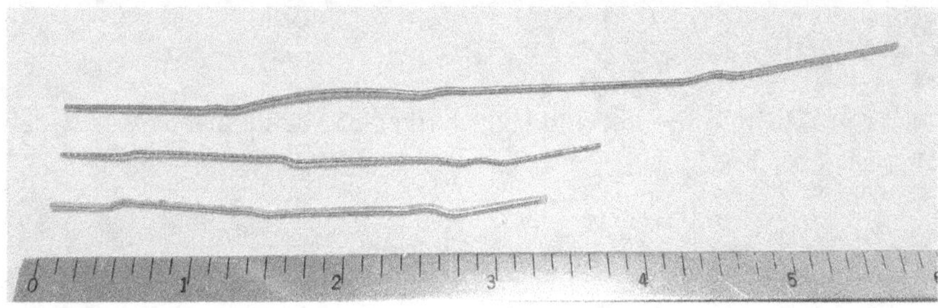

If you have to cut your wire, we recommend cutting a 5 inch (13 cm) piece and looping half an inch (1 cm) at each end with pliers to prevent sharp edges from damaging the filter material or causing a hazard to your face.

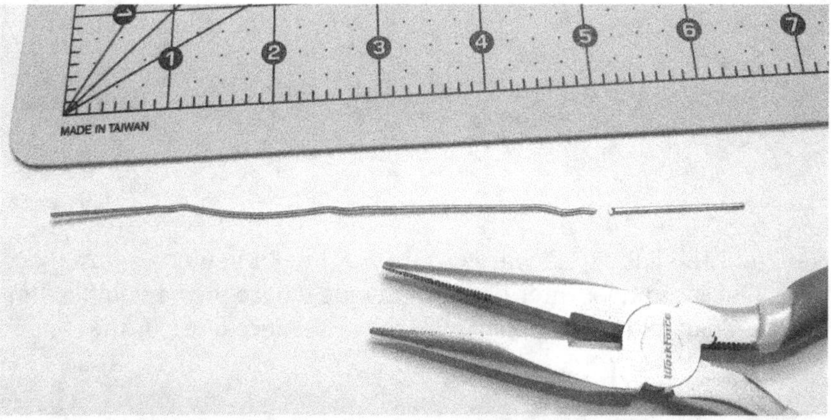

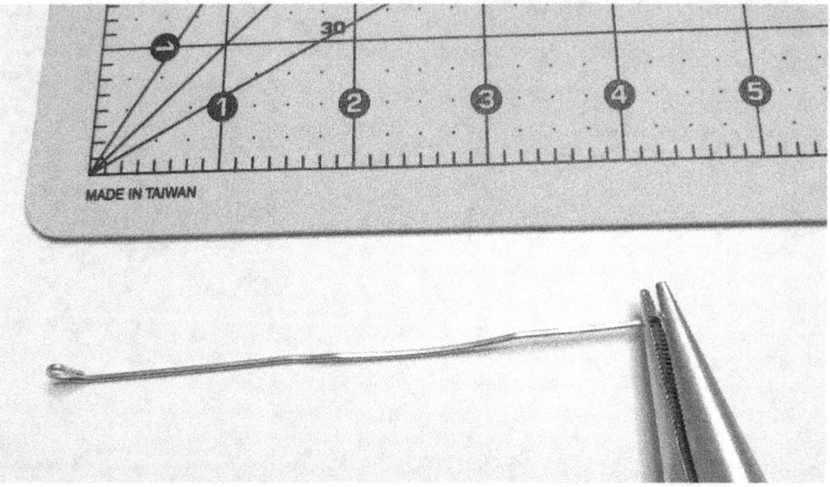

Assembly

To assemble, fold the left and right halves of the square over to meet at the center line.

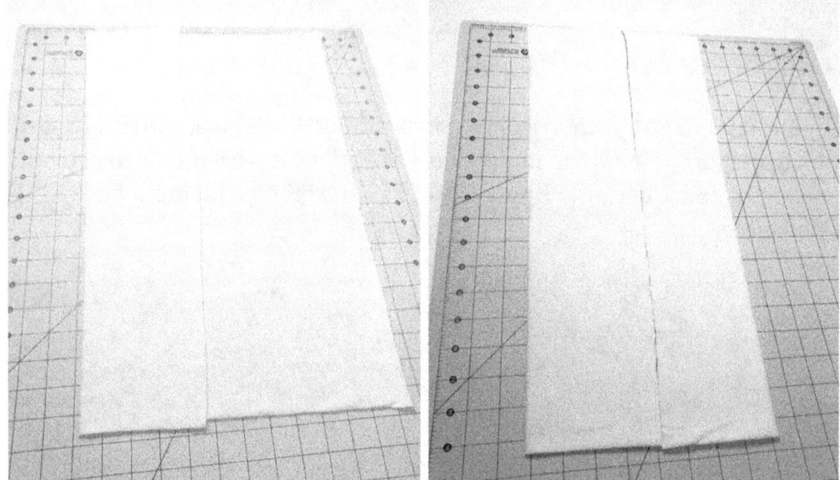

Now fold the left side inwards a second time. If you use a nosepiece wire, place it in the center of the right side where the new folded line will be. Then fold the right half over the nose piece towards the center.

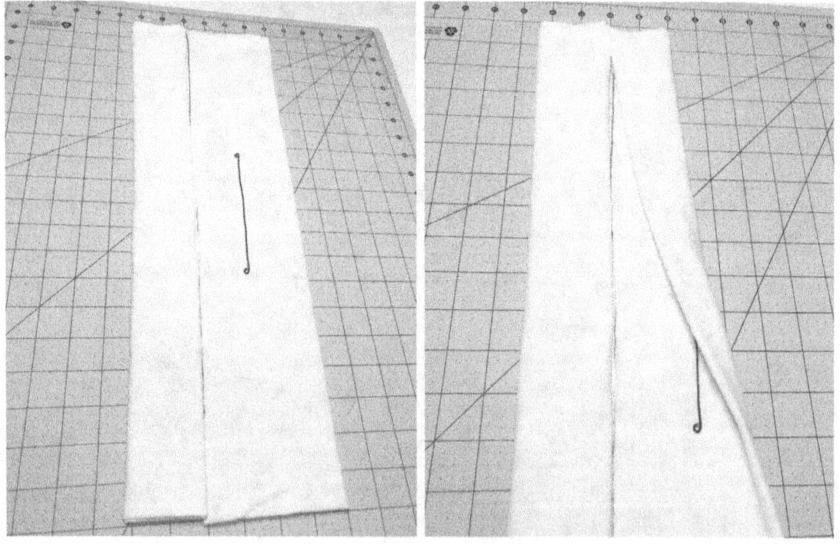

Next, take the first earpiece and slip it over the folded filter material to about a quarter of its length. Repeat this for the other side using the second earpiece.

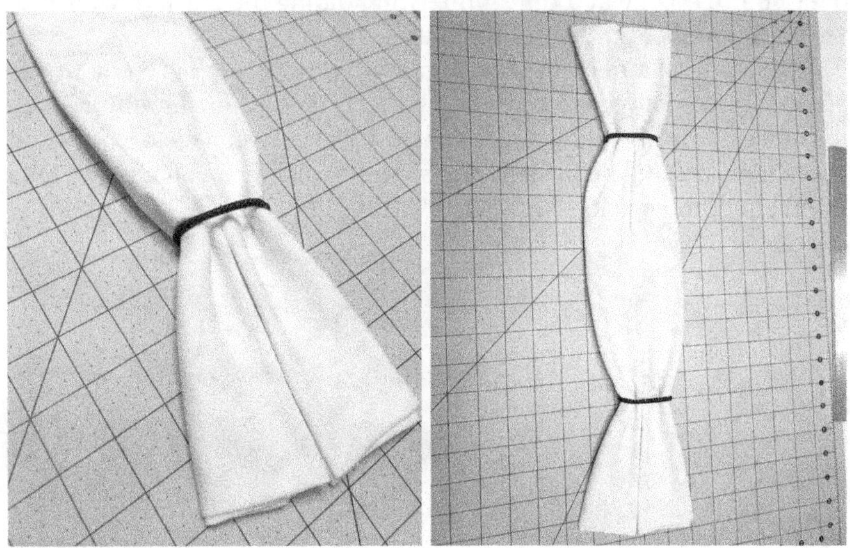

Finally, fold the left and right outer sections inwards so that the earpieces act as fold lines.

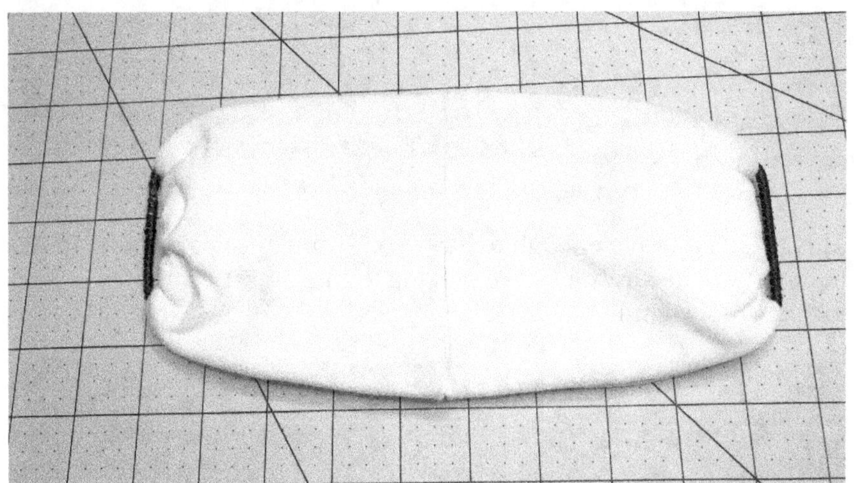

That's it; congratulations on your first mask! Time to try it on. Holding down on the left and right fold lines with both hands, lift the mask up and press it against your face. Then stretch the earpieces back and over your ears one at a time while still holding the mask to your face with one hand. Adjust for optimal fit.

If you added a nosepiece, you can now bend it to perfectly fit the curvature of your nose (ideally at the bridge) and thereby reduce unfiltered airflow coming in through the gap between nose/cheek and mask. This is how the nose pieces should look like if you were to take them out of the masks after proper fitting.

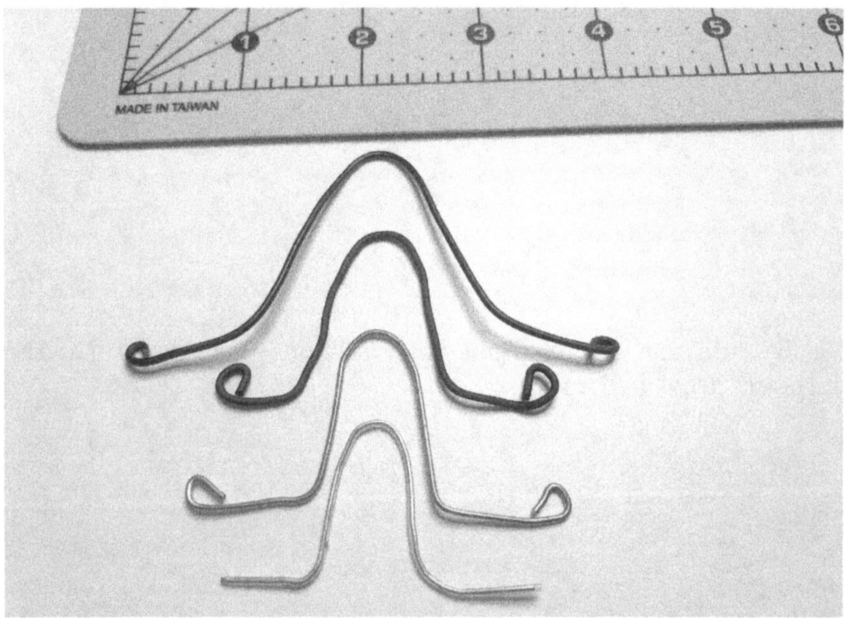

This mask is simple enough to have your little ones participate in the making (and decoration!) of it. Making it a fun and educational activity for the whole family.

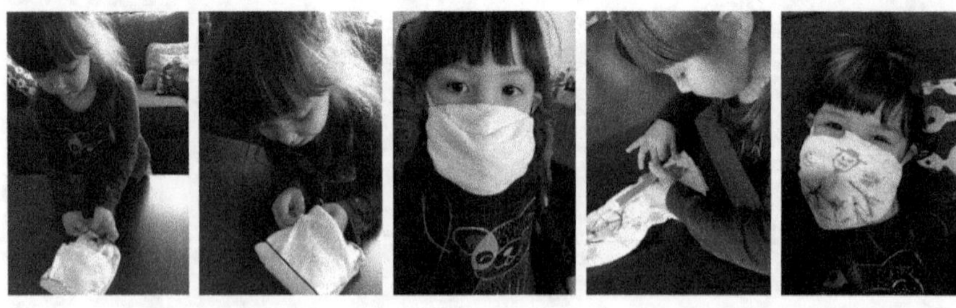

Quick guide to sewing

When we embarked on the journey to make our own face masks, we noticed quickly that following even the simplest sewing instructions requires a good understanding of sewing and knowledge of sewing terminology. We therefore tried to use verbiage in our instructions that is understandable to everyone, as well as used more pictures than most other instructions. This might feel out of place or even unprofessional to some of our readers that possess more advanced sewing skills but was necessary to make these instructions accessible for everyone.

Despite our best efforts, we still must use several sewing terms in our explanations and want to briefly explain these below. For further explanation of sewing terms, please refer to guides on the internet. A good one we like is: https://crazylittleprojects.com/sewing-dictionary-with-pictures/.

- Right side vs. wrong side: When we mention the "right side", we are referring to the printed or nicer side of the fabric. Consequently, the "wrong side" is the other side of the fabric, where the print and color is usually less visible or faded.
- Right sides together: Usually, we sew things together with right sides touching each other to ensure that the stitching will be on the inside of the finished mask. Putting the right sides together means that you put the two pieces of fabric together in such a way that the right sides are touching each other on the inside and the wrong sides face outside.
- Hem: To make a hem you need to fold the fabric over about 0.5" (1 cm), hold it in place and then fold the fabric over by 0.5" (1 cm) again. There should be no raw edges visible now. Hold in place and stitch to make a hem.
- Lining: This is the inside layer of your mask that is facing towards your face. It is usually not visible to others when wearing the mask as it is "hidden" behind the outer layer.
- Outer layer: The outer layer is the outside of your mask that is seen by everyone else when you wear it. It usually

is the colorful fabric with patterns, vs. the lining that is usually of neutral color and pattern.

- Pin: Pins are frequently used while sewing, they help to hold the fabric in place when you sew. When pinning, it is important to place the pins in such a way that you can still sew through them without hitting the pin.
- Seam allowance: The seam allowance is the width of fabric that is between the stitch you are sewing and the very edge of your fabric. The sewing patterns for the improved mask show the seam allowance with a dotted line. Usually, the seam allowance is 0.5" (1 cm), so you will keep 0.5" (1 cm) of space between the stitch you are sewing and the edge of your fabric.

Sewed face mask with or without filter

What you need

Consumables

Material size below varies depending on the size of the mask, please refer to the size chart in the appendix. The dimensions provided below are for a medium size mask.

- Cover material: Two 7" (18 cm) x 7" (18 cm) piece of cloth from quilted cotton or 100% cotton cloth
- Filter material: Piece of quilted cotton or 100% cotton cloth or an air/vacuum filter that is approved for this usage. The filter is optional as two layers of the cover material already provide filtration
- Earpiece: 8" (20 cm) of elastic sewing band or elastic hair ties
- Nosepiece: 5" (13 cm) crafting or gardening wire

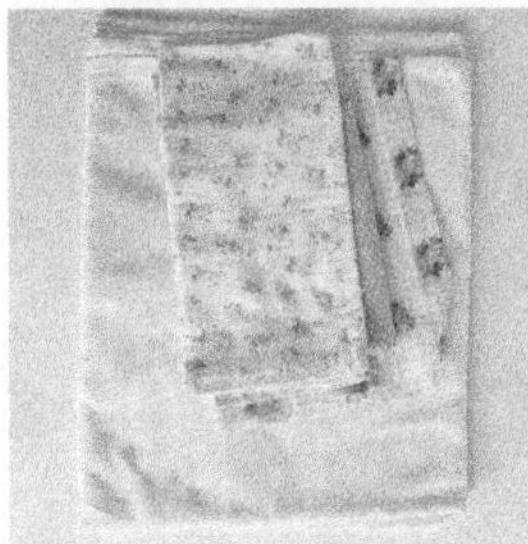

Quilted cotton

100% cotton or cotton mix

Pillowcase

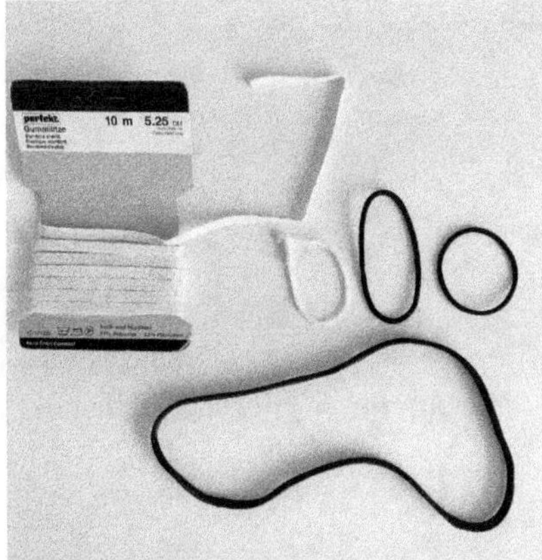

Elastic sewing band or elastic hair ties

Crafting or gardening wire

Note:

- As explained in the disinfection chapter, please remember to use boil-proof cotton for the cover and filter material or pre-boil the material before cutting it into the right size. Boiling the material later without previously having boiled it will make it shrink.
- We recommend using two different colors of cloth for the two pieces you cut out. This is important as the inside is potentially contaminated by your breath and fluids and having two different colors will help you differentiate the sides.

Tools

- Tape measure or ruler, scissors and pencil
- Pins and thread
- Either a sewing machine or a sewing needle; a sewing machine is not a must, but makes the sewing process easier
- Iron and ironing desk; both are optional, but ironing the material makes the sewing process easier and will ensure that the mask looks nice and smooth

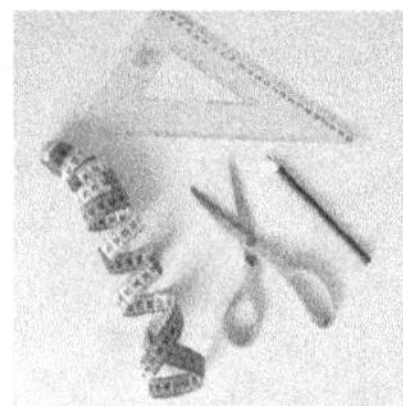   

Tape measure, scissors, pencil and ruler *Pins and thread* *Sewing machine* *Iron*

Assembling the mask

Material size below varies depending on the size of the mask, please refer to the size chart in chapter *Sewing patterns, size chart and further designs*. The material size provided below is for a medium size mask.

Step 1: Cutting and preparing the cloth for your mask

For the instructions, we are using two different pieces of cloth, a white piece for the lining and a white blue striped piece for the outer layer. Iron flat the first piece of cloth.

Mark two 7" (18 cm) x 7" (18 cm) pieces on your material.

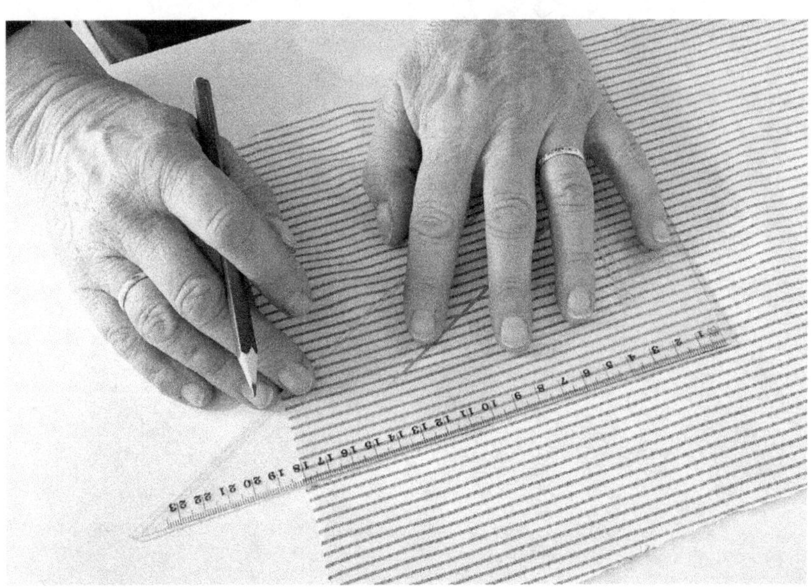

Cut out the marked pieces.

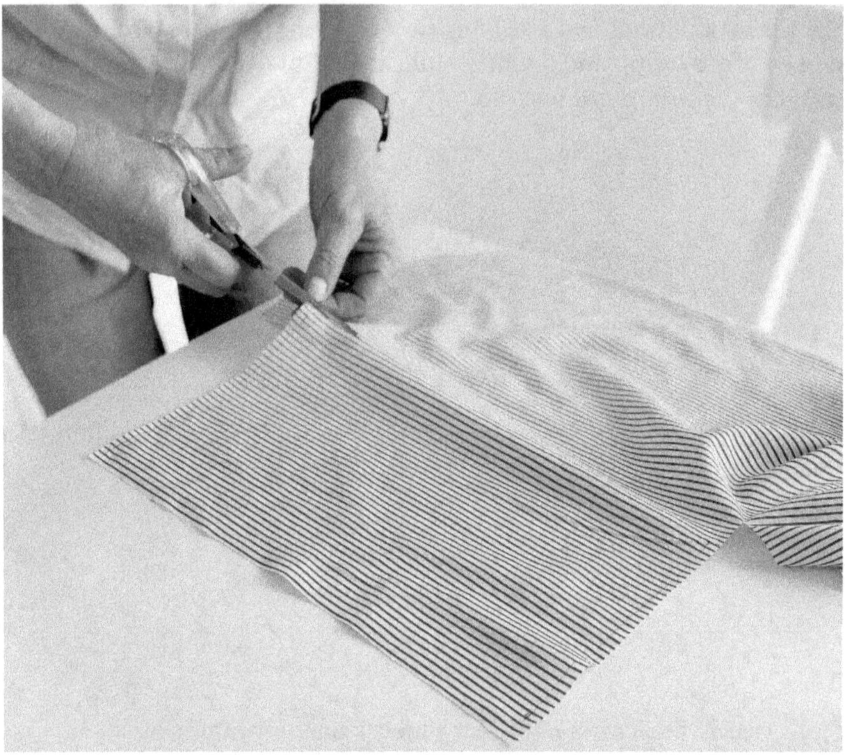

Repeat the same steps for your other piece of cloth.

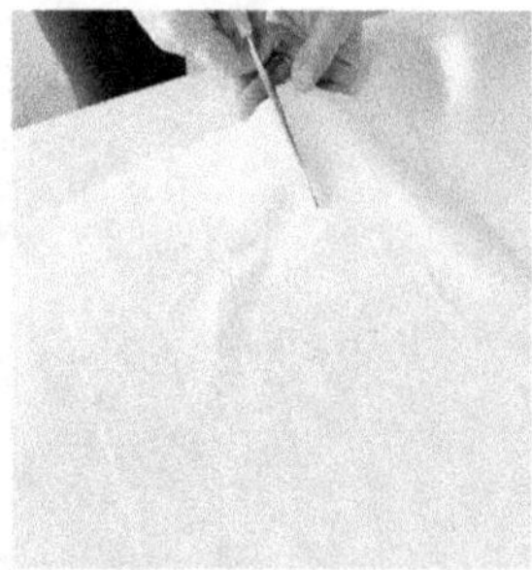

Your cut out piece of cloth should look like this.

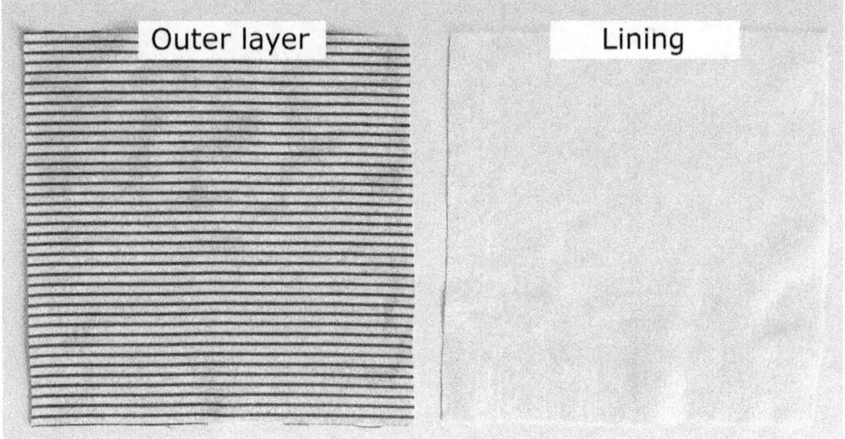

Step 2: Sewing the two mask pieces together

With the right sides (nicer side with stronger color) together, put the two pieces of cloth on top of each other. See below how the right sides are facing inside.

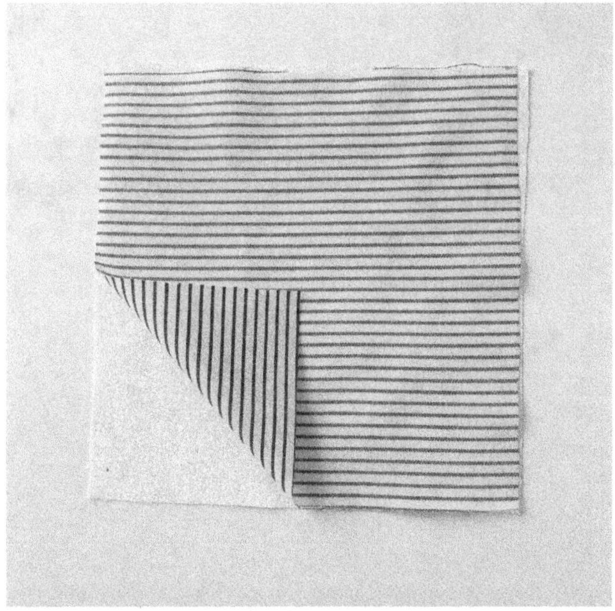

Pin the two pieces together.

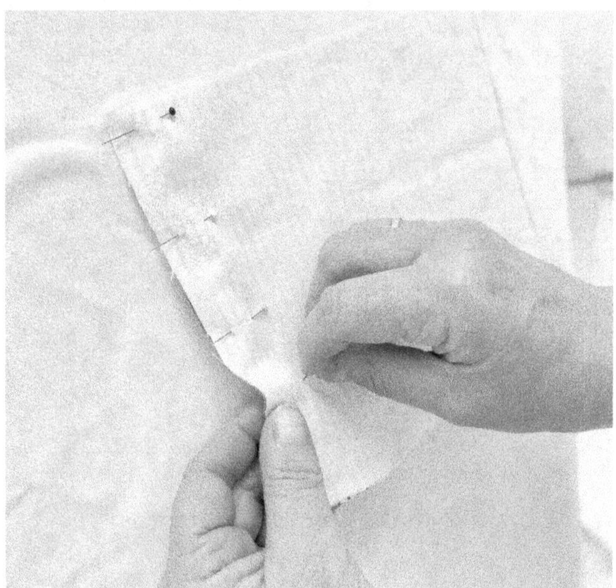

Sew the left and right edges of the two pieces together with a sewing machine or a thread and needle.

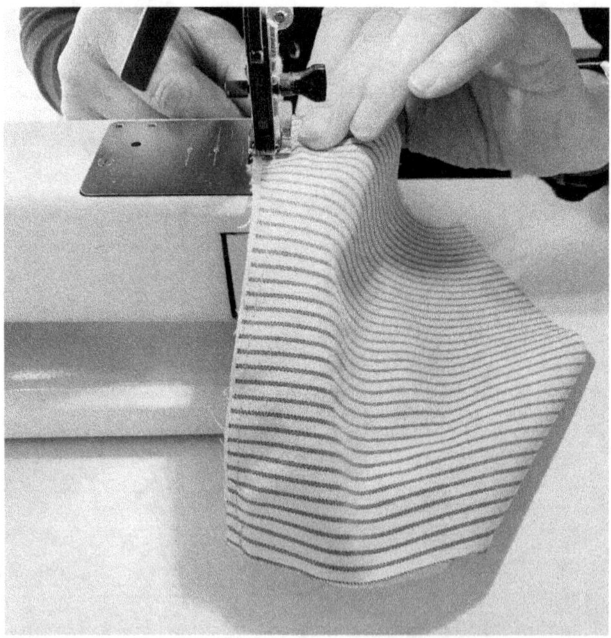

Now reverse the material left to right, so that the inside with the right side is facing outside.

Step 3: Attach the nose piece

The nose piece will allow to smoothly nestle the mask on your nose and ensure a close fit, minimizing aerosol flow. Cut approx. 5" (13 cm) crafting wire and put it into the upper end of your mask and fix it with pins.

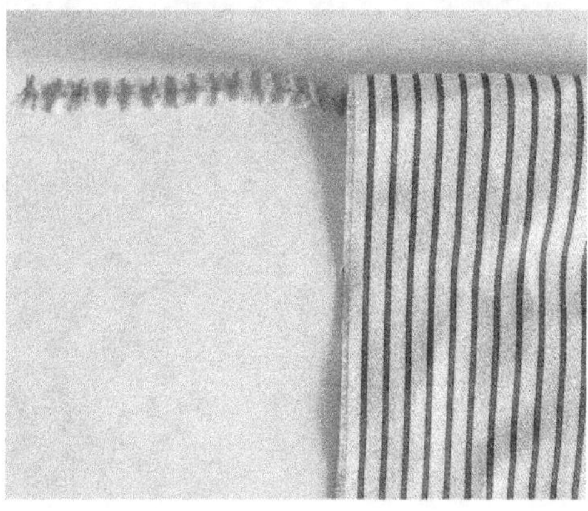

Sew the wire in with a sewing machine or thread and needle.

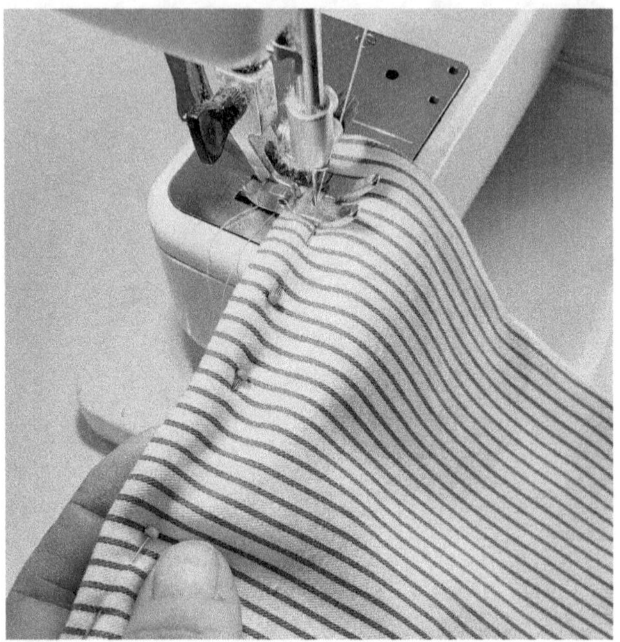

Step 4: Prepare the seam

Iron a hem by folding the seam allowance.

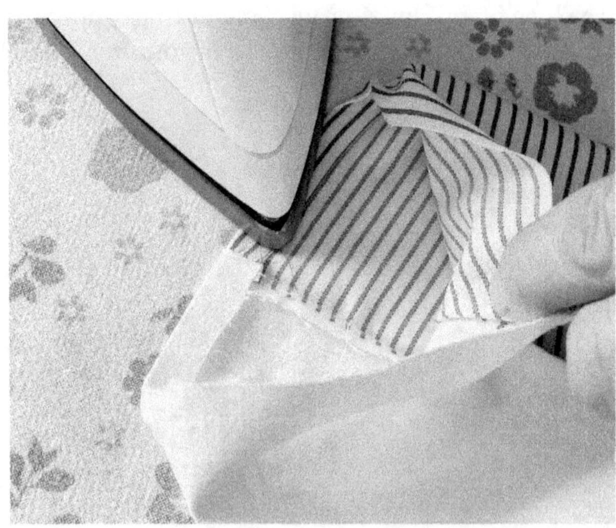

Step 5: Adding pleats for flexibility and face fit

To ensure that the face mask is flexible and nestles nicely to your face contours, you need to add three pleats.

Add three folds, each the depth of approx. 0.5" (1.3 cm) into your mask. Start with the first fold at about 1/3 heights of the mask from the upper side (the side with the nosepiece) down. Hold the folds in place with pins.

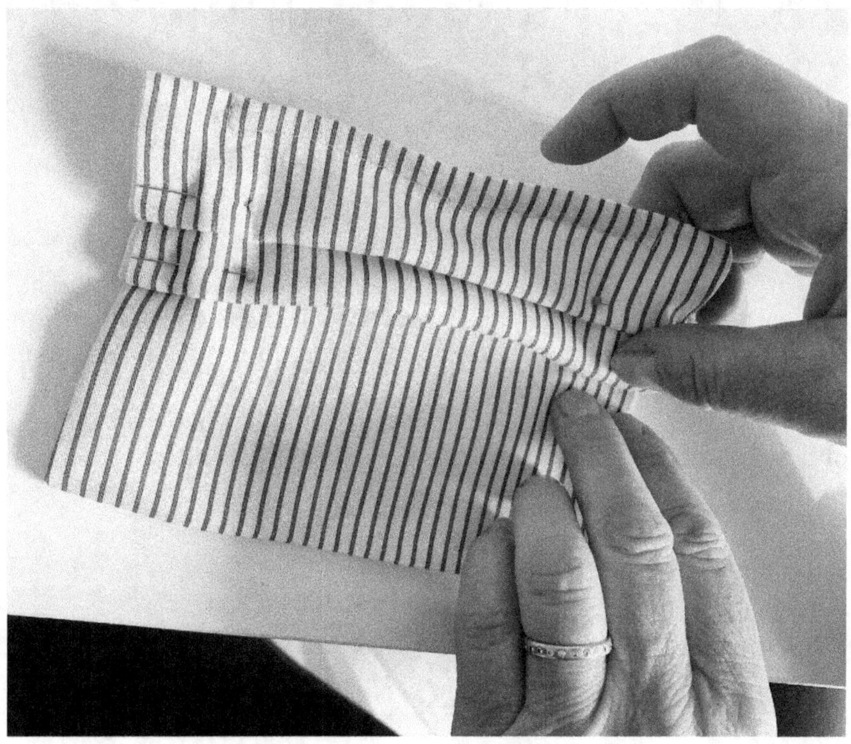

This is how the mask will look like with the three pleats.

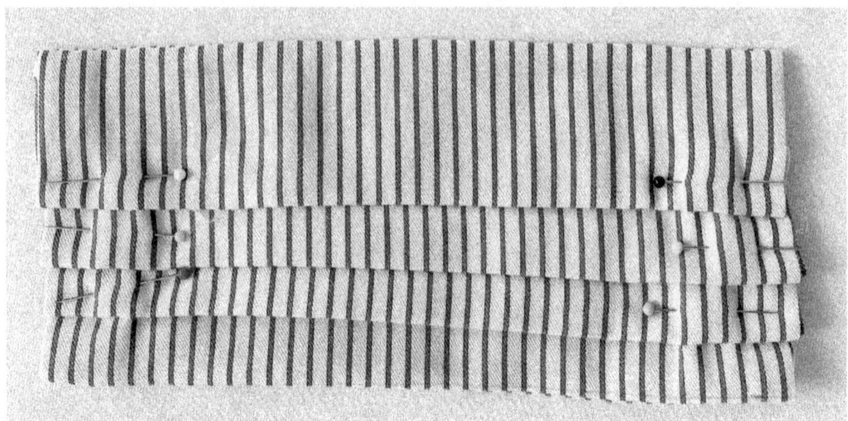

Step 6a: Add the earpiece for mask without filter

The earpiece gives support and ensures your mask will stay well-fit on your face. Follow the steps below if you do not want to use an additional filter.

Cut two pieces of approx. 8" (20 cm) of elastic sewing band. Put one of the elastic sewing bands into the left side of your mask.

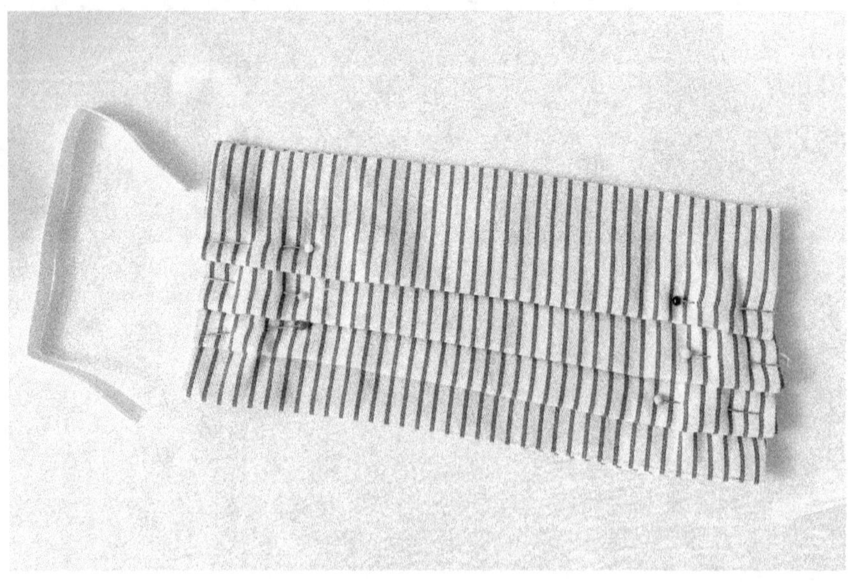

Fix the elastic sewing band on the left side of your mask by sewing the inner and outer layer of cloth together with a hem using a lockstitch. Repeat for the other side.

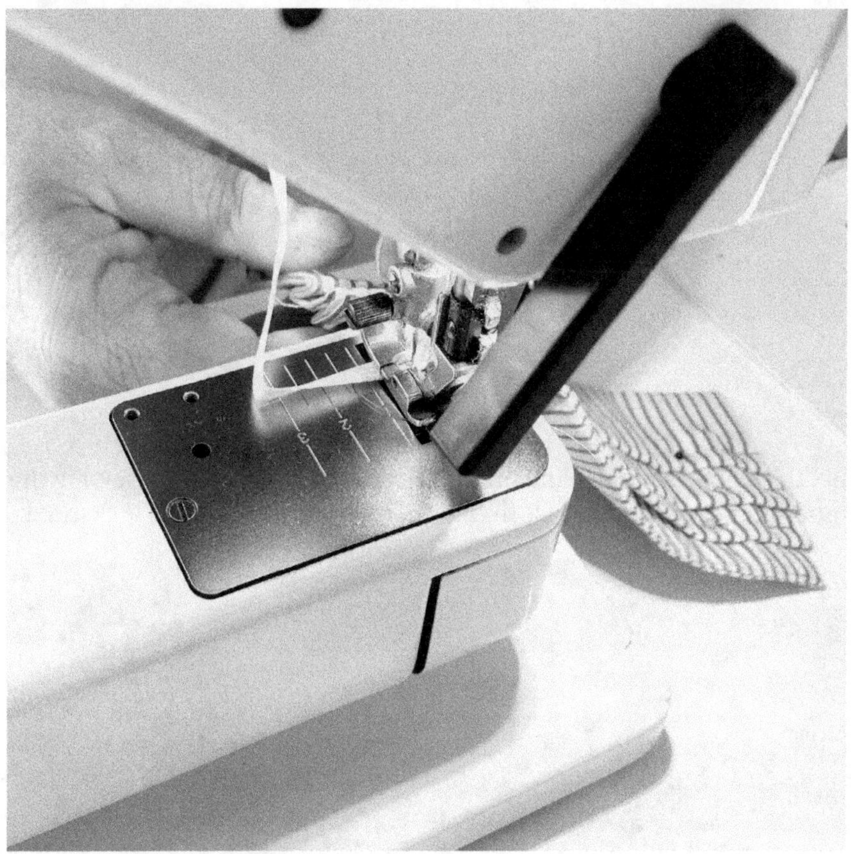

Step 6b: Add the earpiece for mask with filter and add filter

The earpiece gives support and ensures your mask will stay well-fit on your face. Follow the steps below if you want to use an additional filter.

Cut two pieces of approx. 8" (20 cm) of elastic sewing band. Put one of the elastic sewing bands into the left side of your mask.

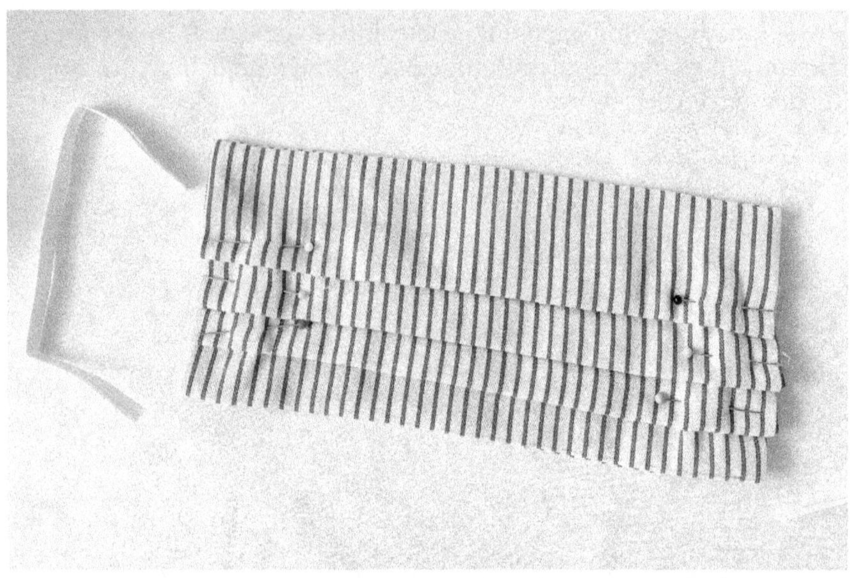

Fix the elastic sewing band on the left side of your mask by sewing the inner and outer layer of cloth together with a hem using a lockstitch.

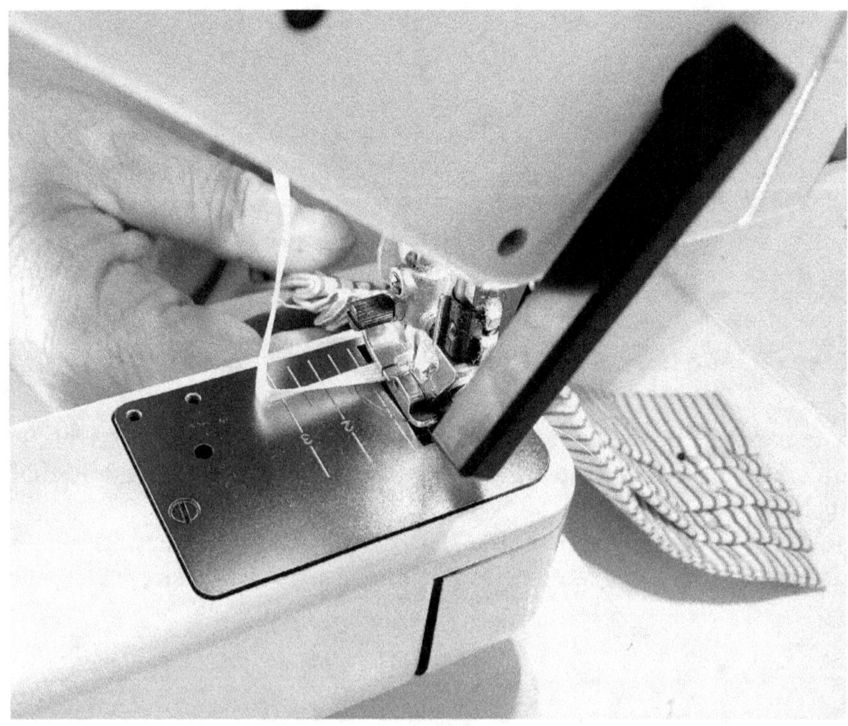

For the right side of your mask you need to leave a tunnel for the filter by sewing a hem using a topstitch around the whole side, without sewing the lining and outer layer of cloth together. Fix the elastic sewing band using an approx. 1 cm lockstitch, keeping the tunnel open. As you are not sewing the lining and outer layer of cloth together, this leaves a pocket on the right side that you can use for a replaceable filter.

Step 7: Your mask is ready

Remove the pins and iron your mask. Iron the pleats as well, so that they fold nicely. Now your mask is ready—well done!

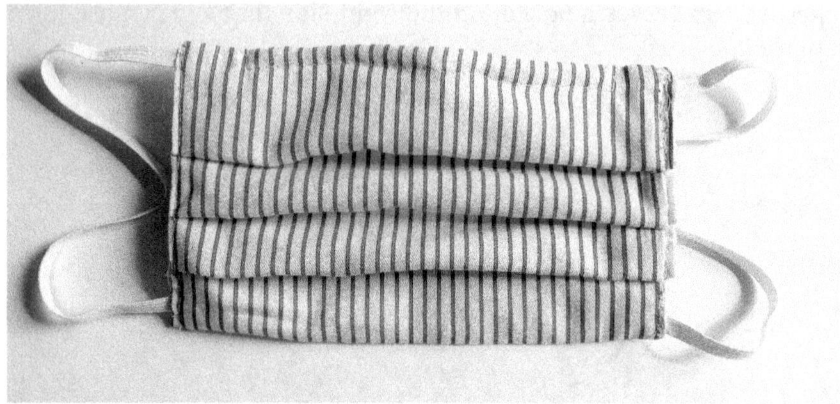

You can see in the picture below, how nicely it bends at the nose piece and can smoothly conform to your face.

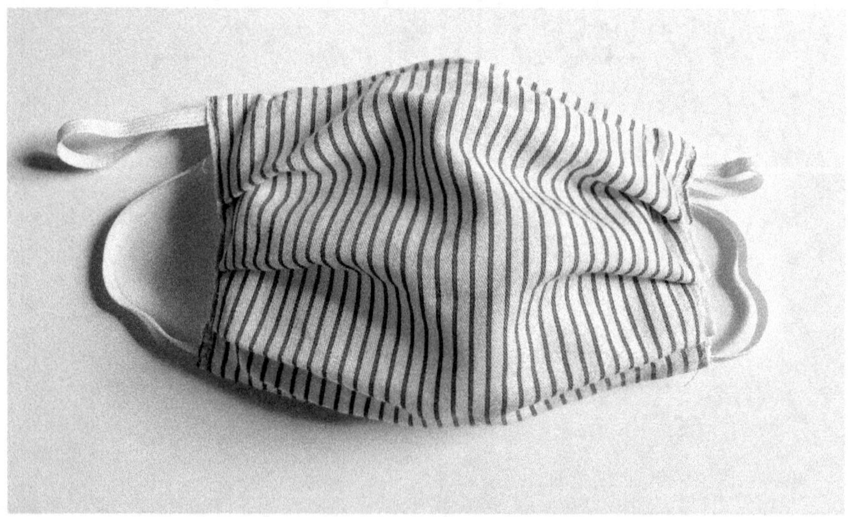

Comparing your sewed face mask with a surgical face mask shows that the main characteristics are similar.

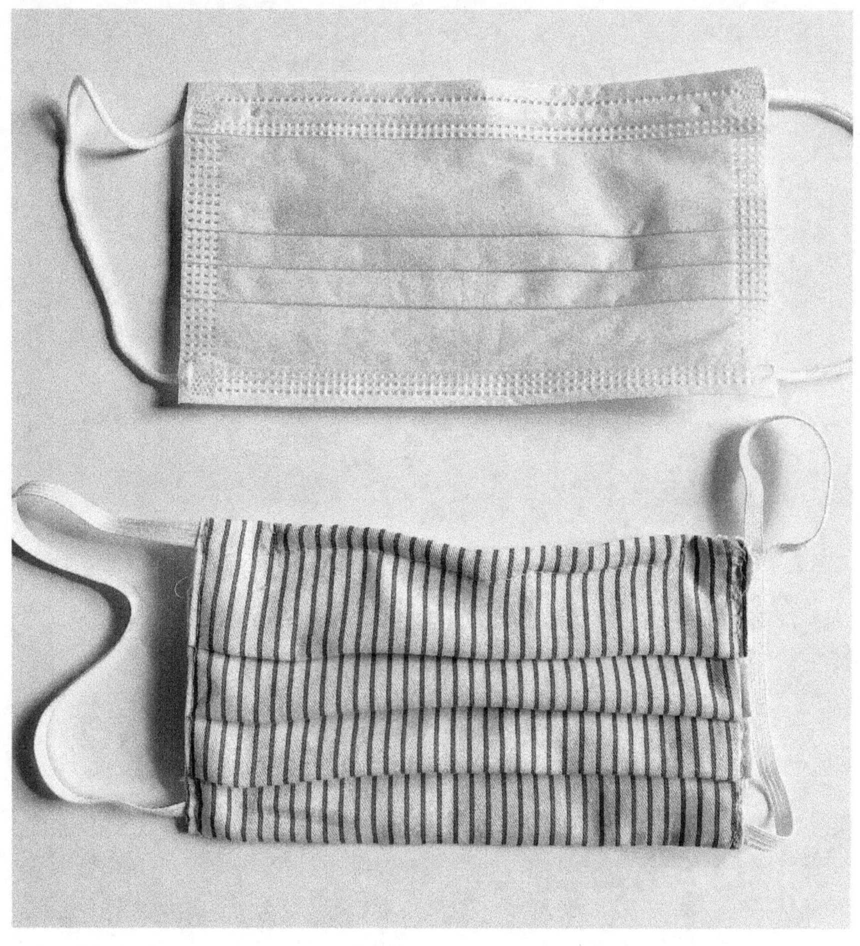

Now you can wear your mask—see the chapter on mask wearing for further details on how to wear and take off your mask.

Improved sewed face mask with or without filter

What you need

Consumables

Material dimensions below vary depending on the size of the mask. Please refer to the sewing patterns in the appendix. The sizes provided below are for a medium size mask.

- Cover material: Two 8" (20 cm) x 8" (20 cm) piece of cloth from quilted cotton or 100% cotton cloth
- Filter material: Piece of quilted cotton or 100% cotton cloth or an air/vacuum filter that is approved for this usage. The filter is optional as two layers of the cover material already provide filtration
- Earpiece: 8" (20 cm) of elastic sewing band or elastic hair ties
- Nosepiece: 4" (10 cm) crafting or gardening wire

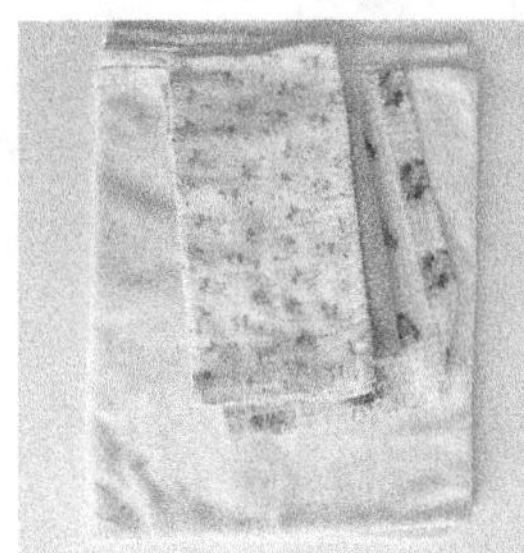

Quilted cotton

100% cotton or cotton mix

Pillowcase

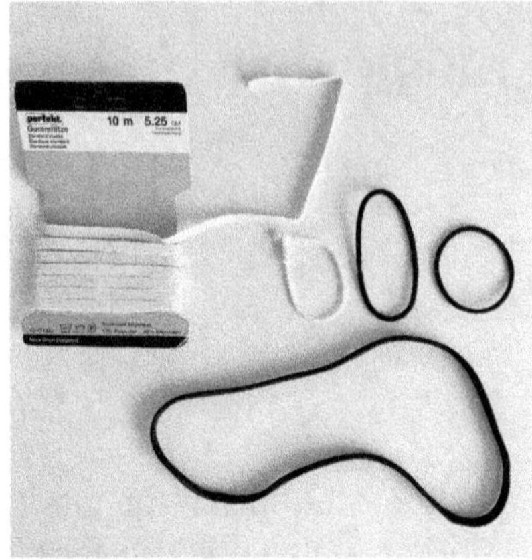

Elastic sewing band or elastic hair ties

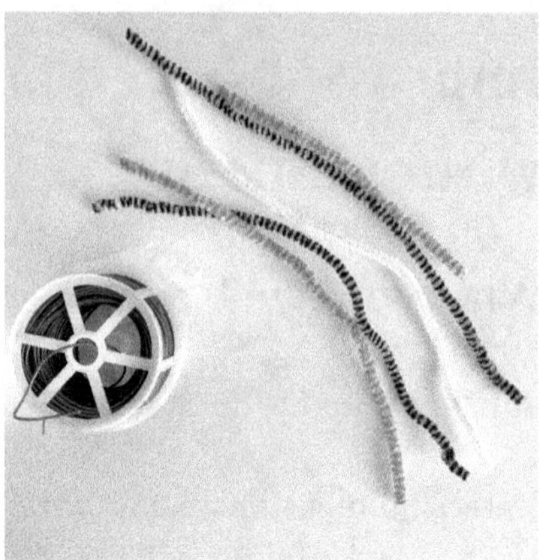

Crafting or gardening wire

Note:

- As explained in the disinfection chapter, please remember to use boil-proof cotton for the cover and filter material or pre-boil the material before cutting it into the right size. Boiling the material later without previously having boiled it will make it shrink.
- We recommend using two different colors of cloth for the two pieces you cut out. This is important as the inside is potentially contaminated by your breath and fluids and having two different colors will help you differentiate the sides.

Tools

- Tape measure or ruler, scissors and pencil
- Pins and thread
- Either a sewing machine or a sewing needle; a sewing machine is not a must, but makes the sewing process easier
- Iron and ironing desk; both are optional, but ironing the material makes the sewing process easier and will ensure that the mask looks nice and smooth

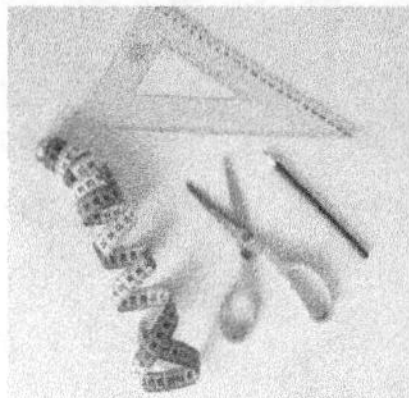   

Tape measure, scissors, pencil and ruler   *Pins and thread*   *Sewing machine*   *Iron*

Assembling the mask

Material dimensions below varies depending on the size of the mask. Please refer to the sewing pattern in the appendix. The material size provided below is for a medium size mask.

Step 1: Cutting and preparing the sewing pattern

Follow the link in the appendix to download the sewing patterns. Print the sewing patterns (make sure to keep the original image size when printing from your PDF reader). Cut out the two components of sewing pattern for your size, adult M in our example, along the solid line.

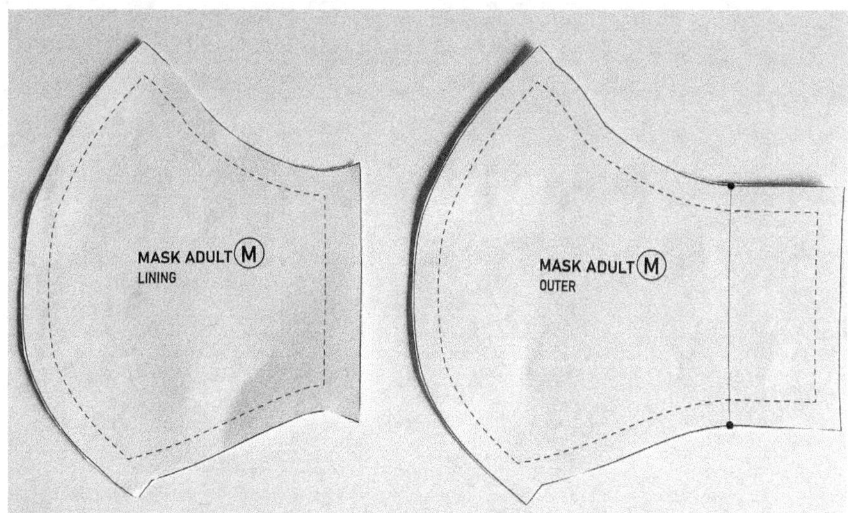

Step 2: Cutting the face mask pieces

For the instructions, we are using two different pieces of cloth, a white piece for the lining and a blue piece for the outer layer. Iron flat both pieces of cloth.

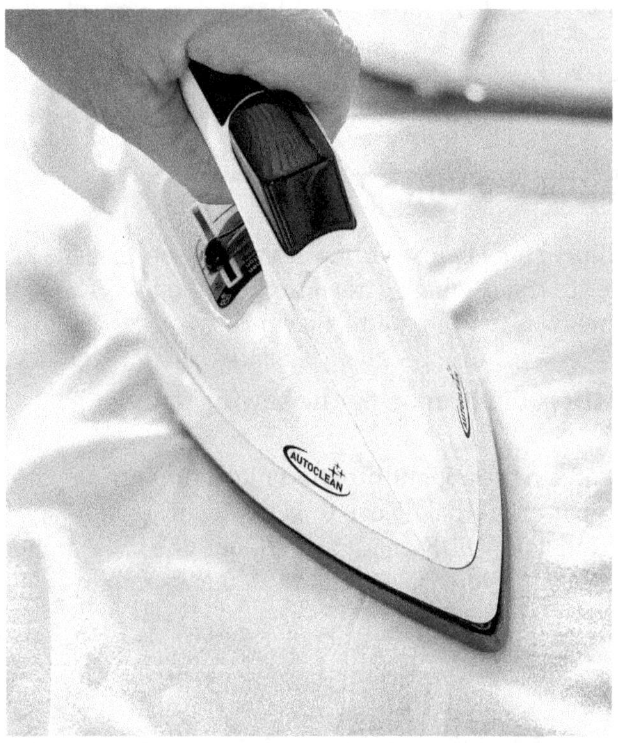

For the outer layer, fold your piece of cloth in the middle, so that the right sides (the nicer side) are together. Put your outer layer sewing patterns on the folded cloth and pin the three layers (2 layers of cloth and 1 layer of sewing pattern) together, making sure the pins go through both layers of cloth, and cut out both layers along the sewing pattern.

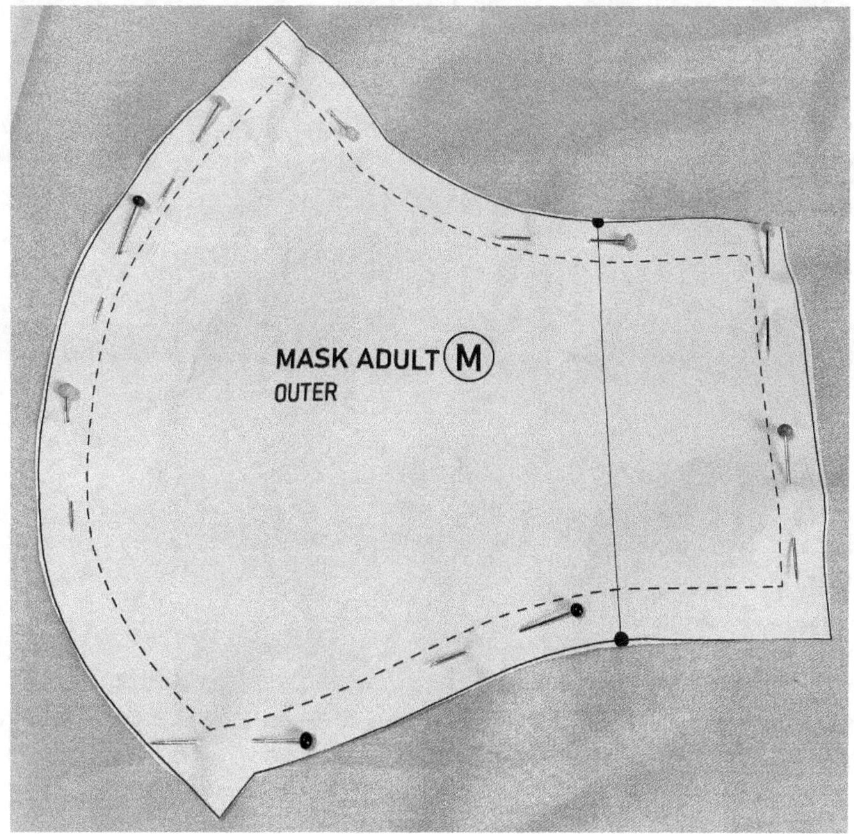

You now have two mirrored pieces of the outer layer. Repeat the same steps for the lining. You now have four pieces of cloth, two for the lining and two for the outer layer. If your pieces of cloth are wrinkled after the cutting process, like ours in the picture below, then you can iron them again.

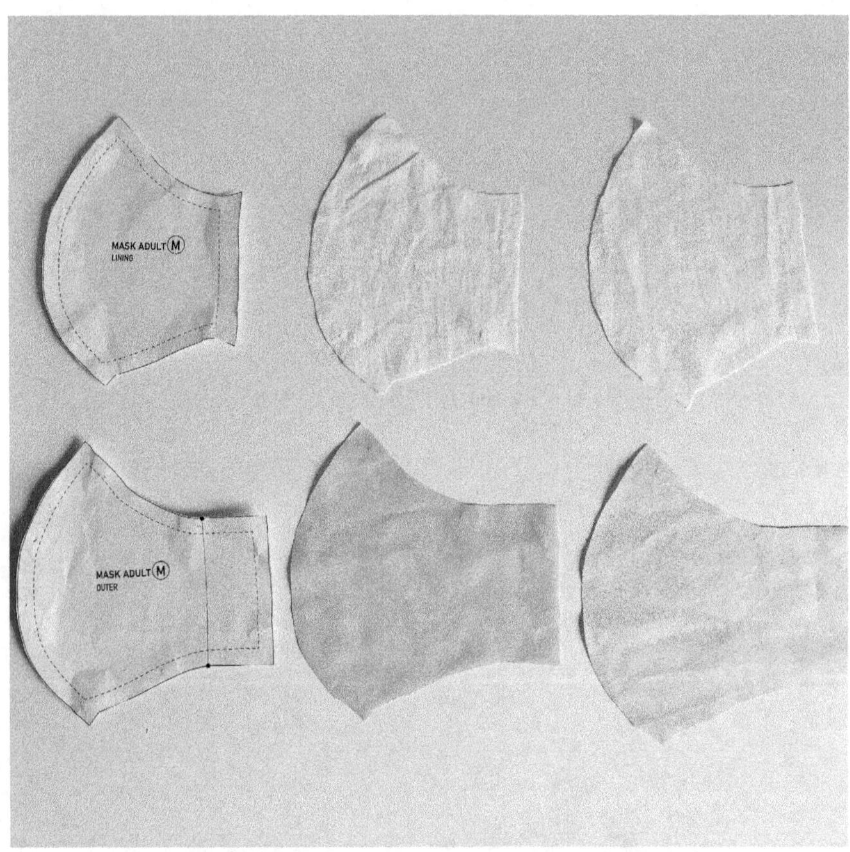

To make the remaining steps in the instructions easier to follow, we explain the components briefly below.

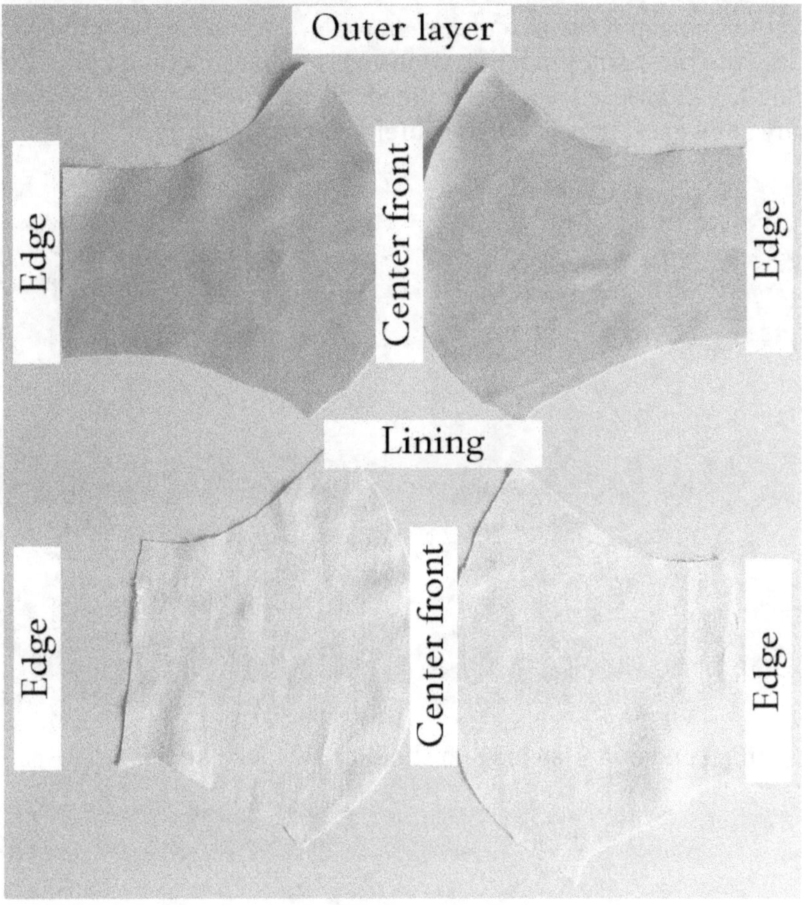

Step 3: Sew the pieces for each side together along the center front

For the lining, put the two pieces on top of each other, with the right sides (the nicer side) together. Optionally, you can fix with pins. Sew along the curved edges of the pieces using a 0.25–0.5" (0.5–1 cm) seam allowance. Repeat for the outer layer cloth pieces.

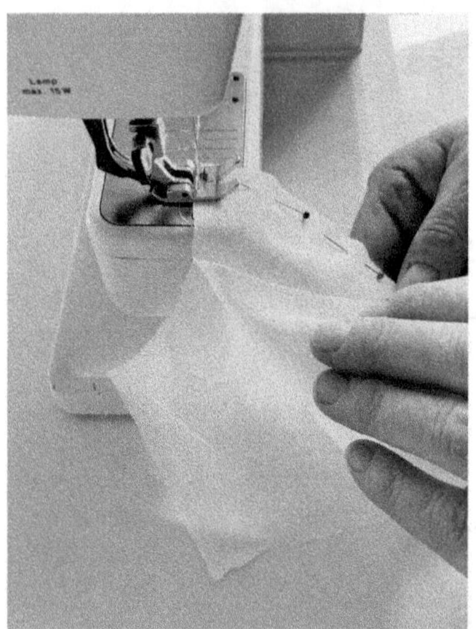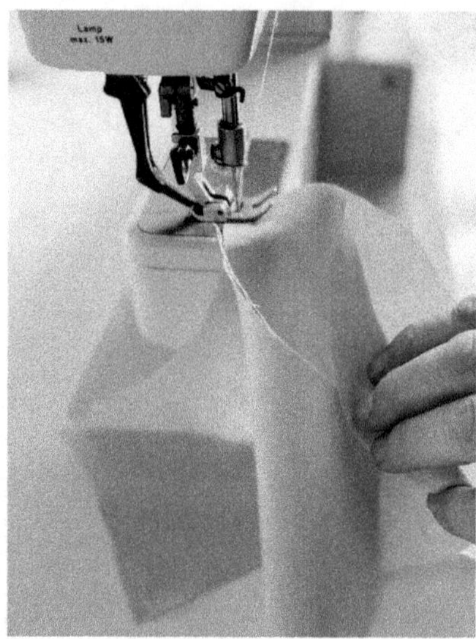

The lining and outer layer seam should now look like this.

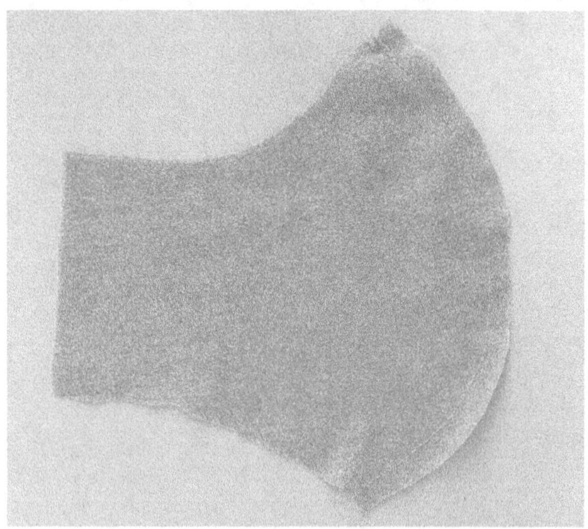

Step 4: Cut out corners, iron and reverse

Optionally, you can cut out corners on the rounding of the lining and outer layer to allow for easier ironing. Make sure you do not cut into the seam.

Iron the center front seam allowance towards the right side. Using the pointed edge of an ironing board makes this easier. Reverse the material, so that the inside with the right side is facing outside.

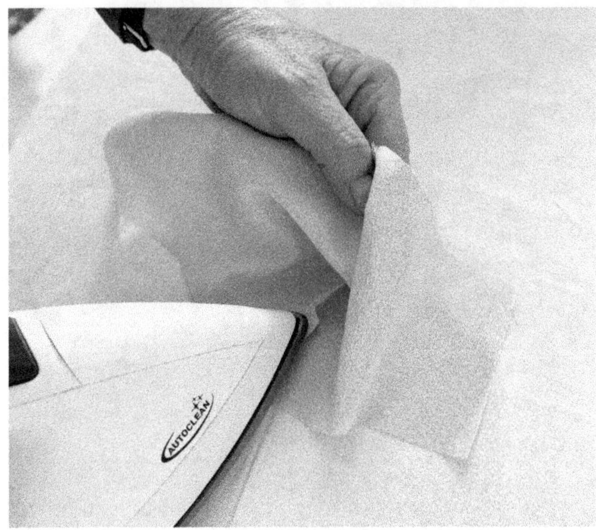

Repeat for the other piece of cloth. This should now look like this.

Step 4: Sew a tunnel for the earpiece

Fold up the outer layer cloth again. For both sides of the outer layer, use the sewing pattern to mark a straight line for the earpiece tunnel.

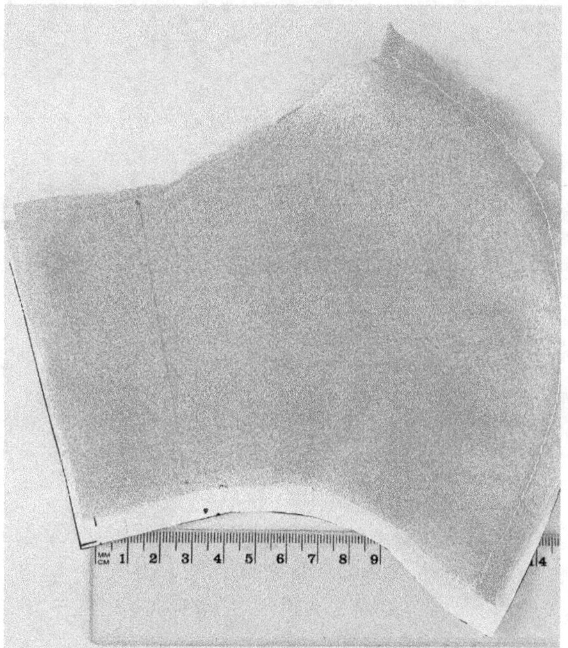

Fold two corners into each edge of the cloth, folding up to the line you marked in the previous step. Iron flat the corners.

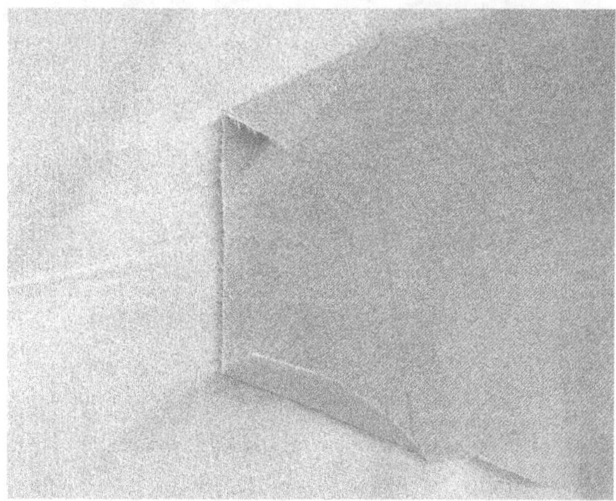

Fold the corners two times at each side up to the line you marked. Fix with pins.

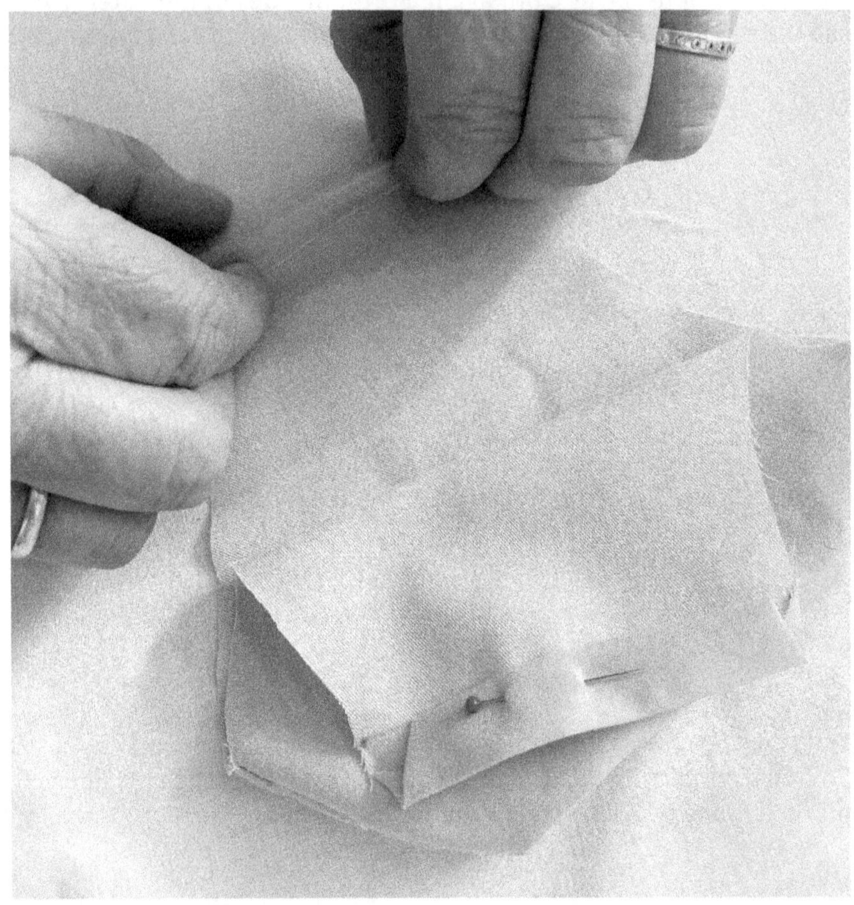

Iron the tunnel.

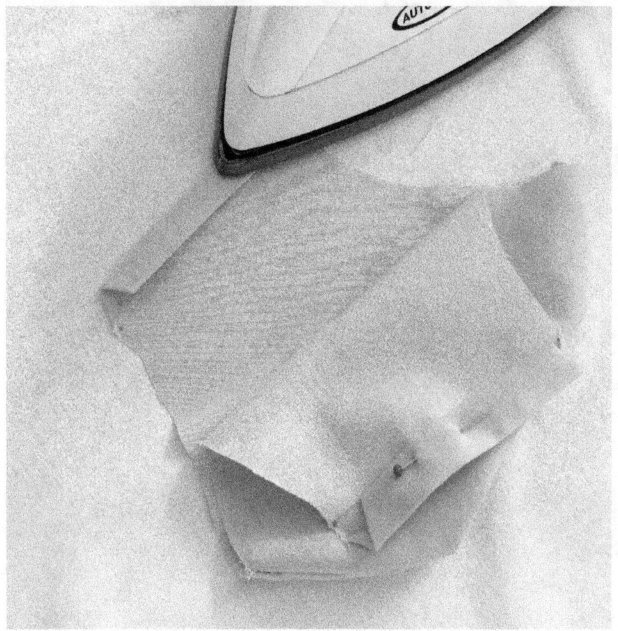

Sew the tunnel.

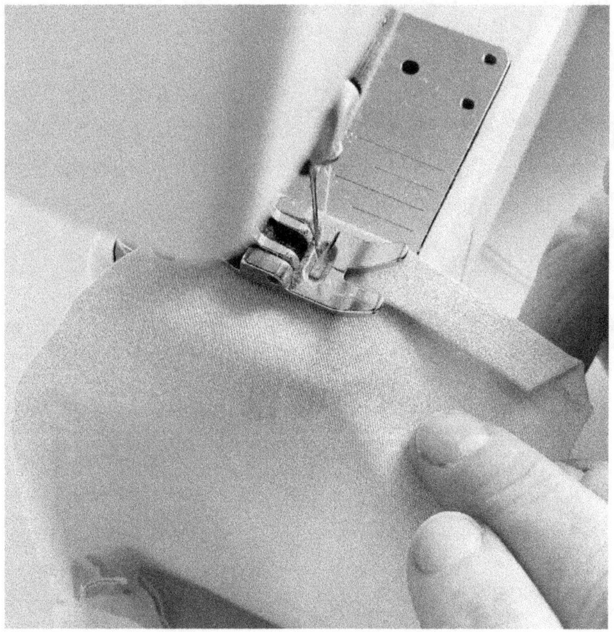

The tunnels now look like this.

For the lining layer, fold the cloth at each edge at around 0.2"–0.3" (0.5–0.7 cm). Fix with pins.

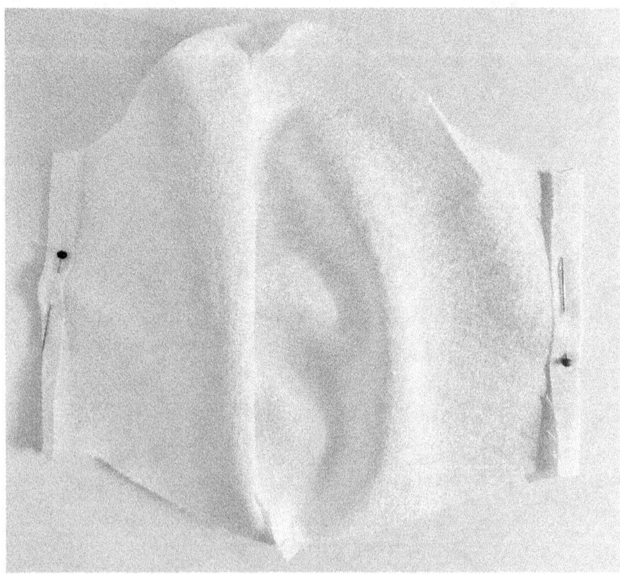

Sew the folded edges.

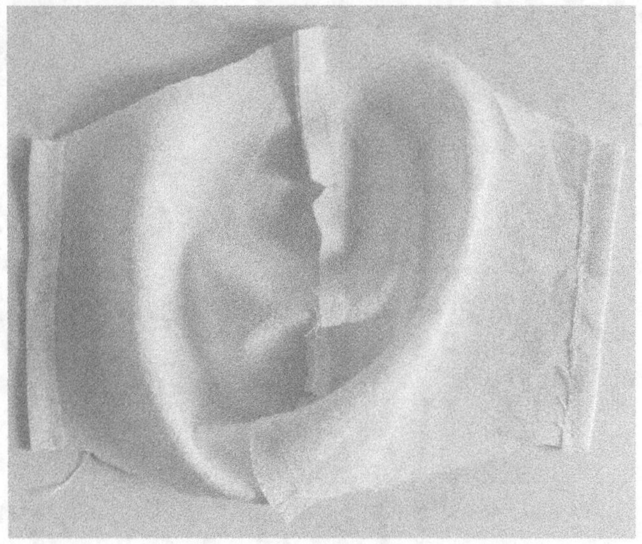

Step 5: Sew the lining and outer layer of your mask together

With the rights sides together pin the lining and outer layer of your mask together. Pin from the center front seam allowance to the right and left.

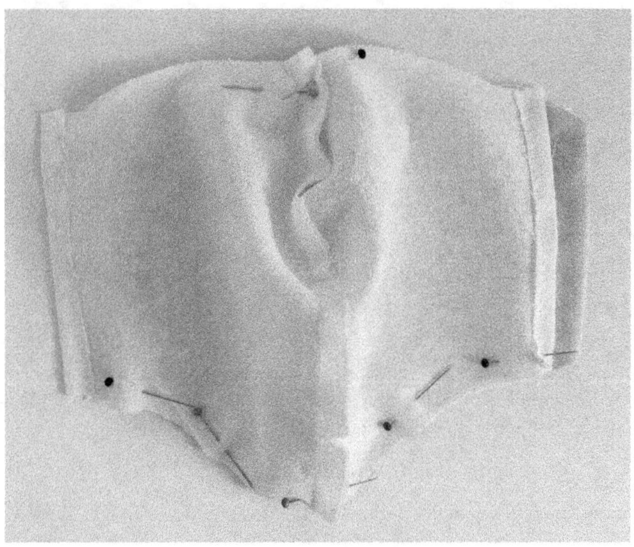

Sew the pieces together. Be careful to not sew into the tunnel.

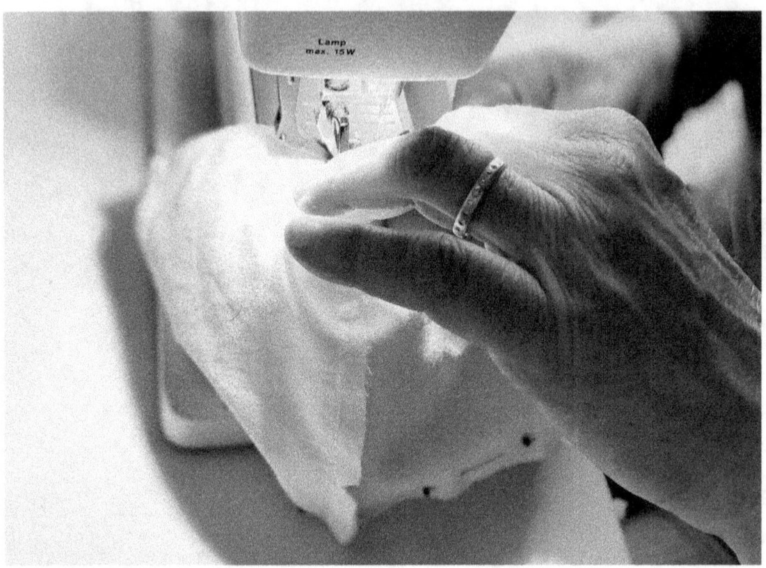

See how we left the tunnel open.

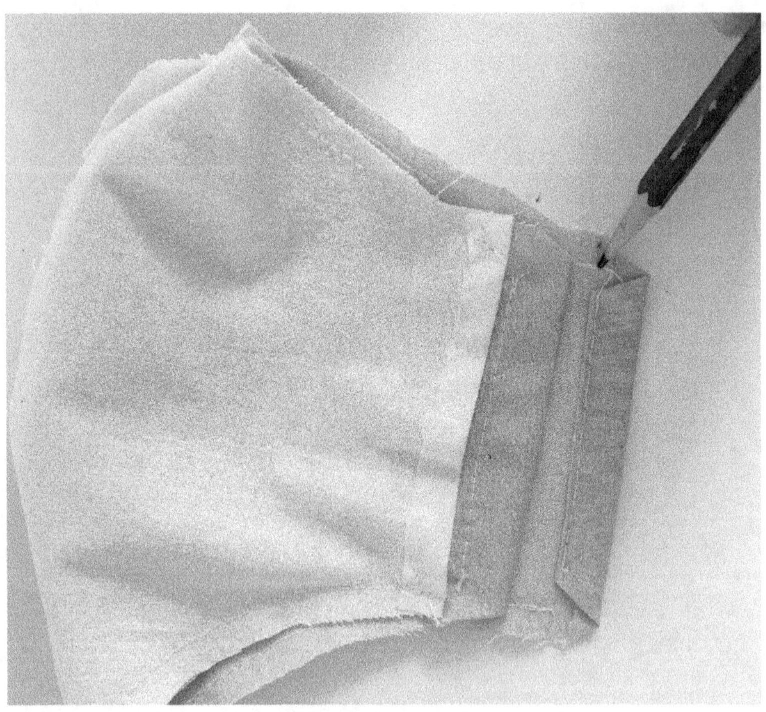

Now reverse the material left to right, so that the inside with the right side is facing outside.

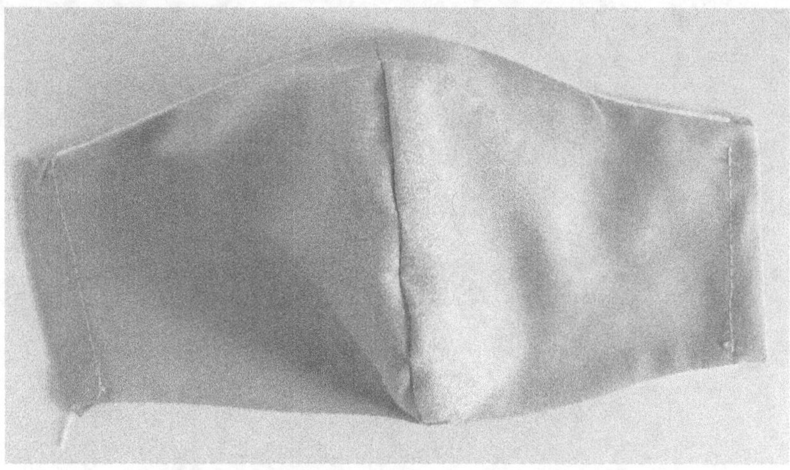

Step 6: Sew the top together using a topstitch

Sew the top together using a topstitch.

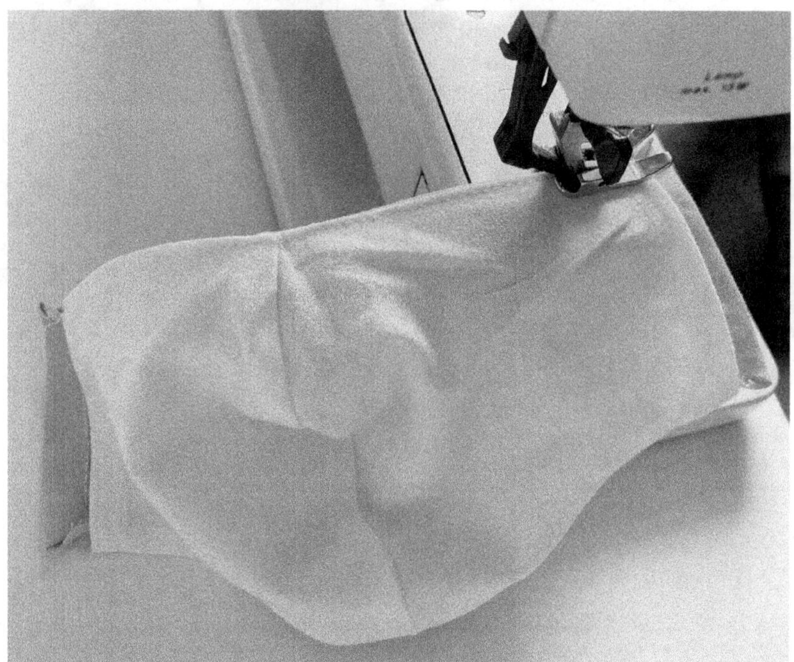

This should now look like this.

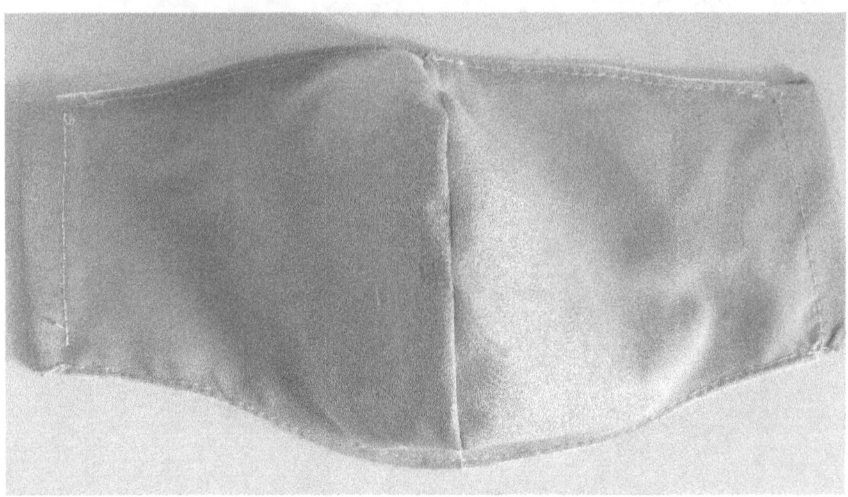

Step 7: Sew the nosepiece

The nose piece will allow to smoothly nestle the mask on your nose and ensure a close fit, minimalizing aerosol flow.

On the top of the mask, you need to sew a tunnel for the nosepiece. Use a pin to mark the tunnel, at around 2.2" (5.5 cm) from the center front seam to the left and right side.

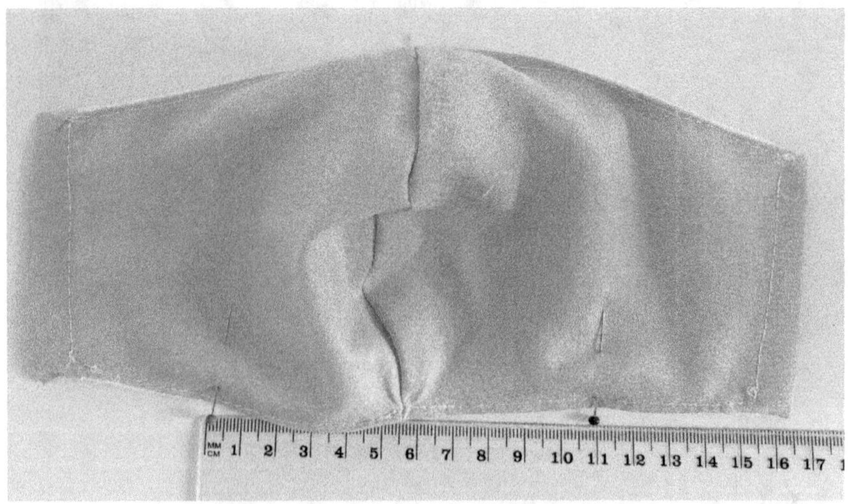

Sew the tunnel for the nosepiece between the two pins (4.4" [11 cm] in length).

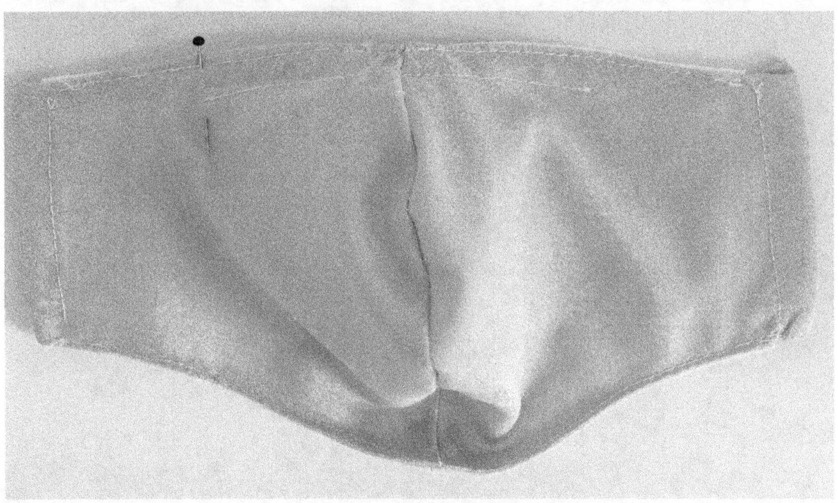

Use around 4" (10 cm) of wire as nosepiece and put it into the tunnel. Ensure you bend and loop any sharp edges.

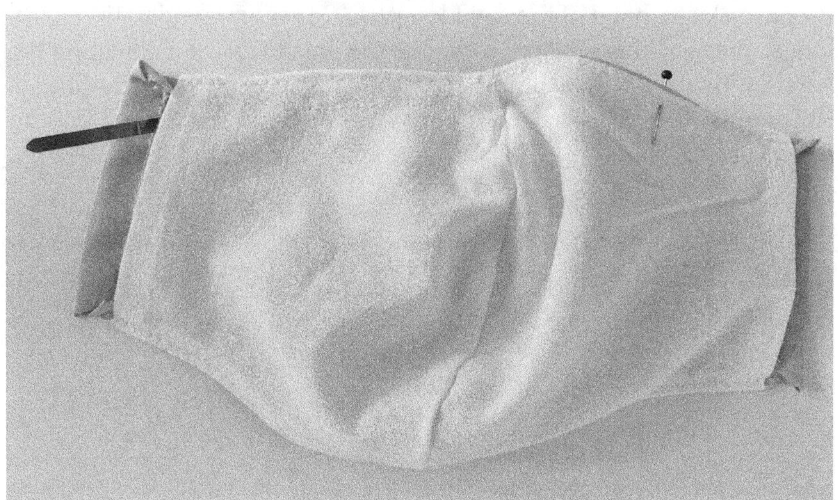

Sew the tunnel.

Step 8: Add the earpieces

Prepare elastic band of the right lengths. We recommend to first use a longer piece of elastic band, trying on the mask and then adjusting the lengths. Using a safety pin, thread the elastic band into the tunnel. Now adjust the lengths again to the wearer's head and make a knot to fix the elastic band.

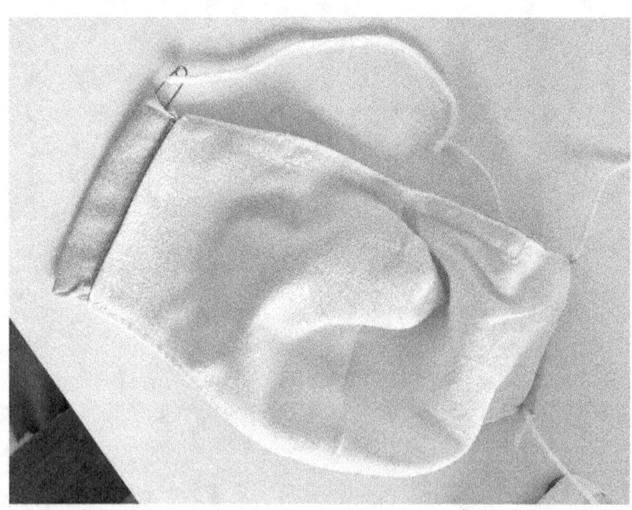

Optionally, you can put a filter into the filter pocket. Either a square-shaped filter or you can use the sewing patterns to cut out a filter in a shape that best fits your mask.

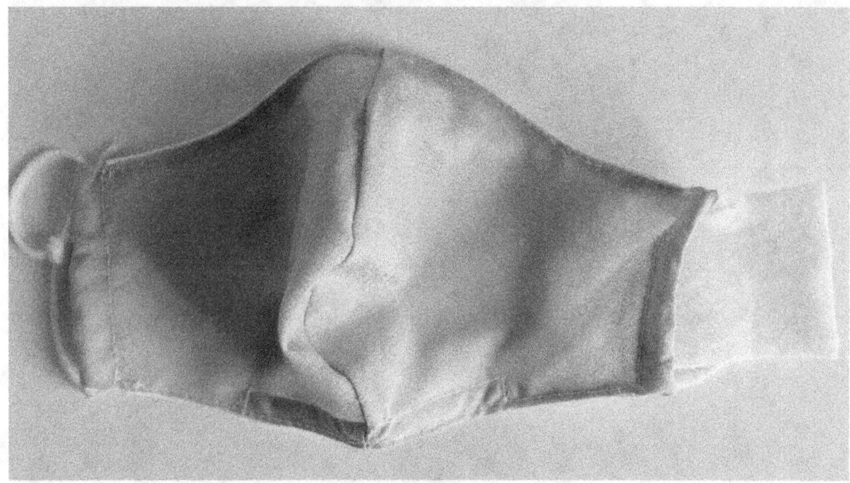

This is how the finished mask looks like. Our user experience with the improved sewed mask is that the bulge of the mask allows for air to circulate easier and thus makes breathing feel more natural. Thus, we feel that breathing is easier with this model, when compared to the simple sewed mask.

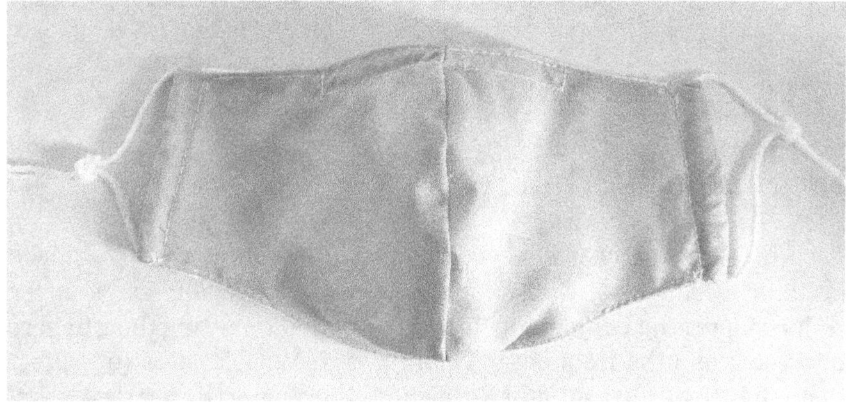

Now you can wear your mask—see the chapter on mask wearing for further details on how to wear and take off your mask.

Face masks for children and pets

Face masks for children

The CDC recommends children 2 years and older to wear a cloth face mask, covering their nose and mouth.[53] Especially as younger children have the habit of touching their face and putting their fingers into their mouths frequently, wearing a face mask helps to protect them and their surroundings. But note that generally masks of any kind should never be worn by children younger than 2 years because of the risk of suffocation, as well as any person with known breathing problems.

Making a face mask for kids is easy. Just follow the steps outlined in the mask designs above (refer to previous section) and adjust the size according to the size chart for your children. However, getting a child, especially a toddler, to wear a face mask, keep it on, and refrain from touching it all the time will be more difficult. Below, we provide you with a few tips to make it easier to convince your little ones to wear a mask:

1. Use kid-friendly designs, such as a cloth with their favorite movie character, an animal print or a color and pattern they like. Allowing kids to choose their own material will also get them more excited. One of the authors' 2-year-old daughter, for example, chose the rose flower pattern below, which is printed on a very soft 100% cotton material. She really likes wearing it and finding matching outfits. Also allowing your kids to participate in your do-it-yourself face mask project will help them see this as a fun activity with their loving parents (and any siblings).

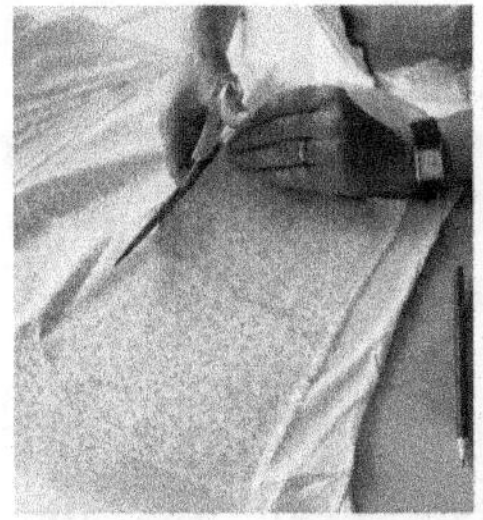

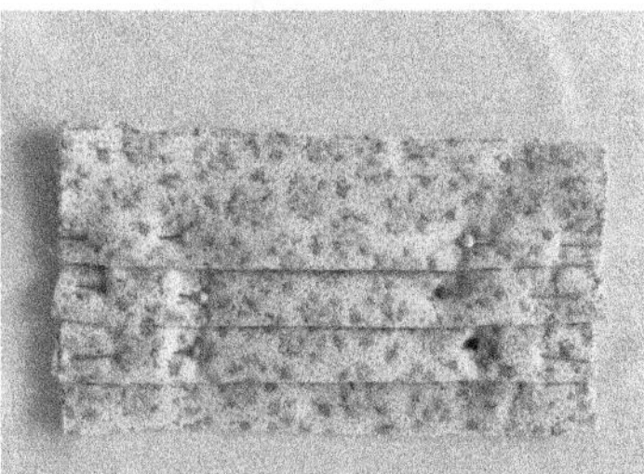

2. Explain to your kids, in a child-friendly manner, what the coronavirus is and why it is important for them to wear a face mask. You will certainly receive a lot of questions from your kids about why they cannot go to play dates and their daycare or school facility. That said, you probably have already done a lot of explaining. That means your children may have some level of understanding for what is going on and might be receptive to your reasoning for wearing a face mask in public.

3. Lead by good example and make wearing the face mask fun. If you and the rest of your family or loved ones regularly wear a mask, then it becomes natural for your children to feel motivated in wearing masks as well. You can even build a ritual around it, like putting on the mask whenever putting on shoes to go outside. We have built some play into the process, having multiple masks for each of us and matching colors and patterns to our outfits. All family members or loved ones having matching colors and patterned masks can be an appealing game for your little ones, especially if you build it up in an encouraging way.

4. Use some sort of a reward system, for example praising your child or giving a healthy treat like fruits or a sticker if your child wears the mask.

While this all sounds optimistic and fun, please be realistic and do not expect a toddler to wear a face mask with discipline or for long periods. They will want to touch it, take it off and play around with it, making the whole purpose of wearing a mask useless. So be mindful and limit your child's exposure to others and potentially contaminated surfaces rather than pushing for wearing a mask too hard. It is anyway already a challenging time for children and parents, so do not make it even more difficult. Keep in mind that limiting the child's or children's exposure to others and the amount of time using the face mask has been proven to be the most effective method.

Masks for dogs and other pets

While there is currently not enough data to draw general conclusions, several cases of infected dogs and cats who are living with infected humans have been reported.[54,55] In these instances, the human was likely infected first by human-to-human spread and subsequently passed the virus on to the pet. Since the virus is believed to have already jumped from at least one species to another (bat to human), it is not too surprising that prolonged exposure to infected hosts can eventually lead to other species being infected. However, it is currently unclear whether the infected pets could transmit the disease to other pets or humans. Still, it should be noted that the infected animals did not show signs of illness. Therefore, the actual pet infection rate could be higher than currently assumed. It is therefore prudent to err on the side of caution and protect your pets (as well as others from your pets) to the best of your ability.

Some articles suggest making your pet wear a mask; however, as dog owners, we cannot see how this works, especially if you expect the pet to keep the mask on the whole day. Anyone who ever tried to keep their pet from not touching an alien object, like a bandage, will know from experience that this is very difficult. Thus, getting your pet to wear a mask will be nearly impossible, no matter how good the design is. Thus, we recommend the below for pet owners:

- Keep your pets inside as much as possible.
- If available, use your own private backyard to take your pet for a walk.
- If you must use a public park, always keep your pet on a leash.
- Avoid contact and maintain adequate distance when around other animals (social distancing also works for pets!).

If your pet shows symptoms of illness, call the veterinarian first before going to the practice. In the call, make sure to tell the receptionist whether you are currently infected with the virus or have been infected in the past and have since recovered.

Disinfection of the virus

Since there are various disinfecting agents that are effective against the virus, we can only describe the most common product categories here. Afterwards, we will be looking at some common use cases and share which product category worked best for us in these cases. It should be noted that the US Environmental Protection Agency (EPA) currently lists more than 350 products that can be used to disinfect the virus.

We encourage you to look up cleaning products that you already have at home for comparison with the EPA's website (https://www.epa.gov/pesticide-registration/list-n-disinfectants-use-against-sars-cov-2) to determine if they are effective against the virus.

Effective disinfectants

 Note: Always follow the manufacturer's instructions when using disinfectants. If in doubt, contact the manufacturer directly for more information.

Soaps

The CDC continues to recommend the use of soap and frequent handwashing as one of the most effective disinfection methods for good reasons. It is cheap, simple and effective. Liquid soaps are just as effective as the good old soap bars. Dish washing soap is likewise effective for disinfecting dishes and silverware and so is regular laundry detergent for items that can be washed in the washing machine. There are too many brands and products to list here, but very common products include Softsoap, Meyer's, or Dial for hand soaps, Dawn, Palmolive, or Gain for dish washing soap and Tide, Persil, or Gain for laundry detergents.

Note that we are in no way associated or profit from any of the companies or products mentioned in this book. The stated products were merely chosen based on their broad recognition in the population to help the reader's understanding of these product categories.

For those with skin sensitivities, consider using hypoallergenic and natural or organic products. If in doubt, check with your licensed medical provider. There are now virtual options available for achieving professional medical advice before requiring a physical in-person visit. Consider a phone call consultation, if needed, as a start.

Hand Sanitizers

Similar to the previous category, the CDC recommends the use of hand sanitizers where access to soap and water is not available or impractical. However, due to the high demand in hospitals settings these products must not be bought in excess. The product should either contain at least 60% ethanol or at least 70% isopropanol (also known as isopropyl alcohol or rubbing alcohol) to be effective.[56] Typical brands include Purell and Germ-X.

Disinfectant wipes

This category encompasses wet disposable disinfectant wipes best known from brands like Clorox and Lysol. Care should be taken as some products irritate the skin and require wearing gloves to be used safely. To guarantee maximum effectiveness, always remove any visible dirt or grime from the surface before attempting to disinfect it. Moreover, ensure that the surface stays wet for several minutes as per the product's instructions. Thoroughly rinse disinfected toys and surfaces that will be coming in contact with food. Products in this category are generally only suitable for disinfecting hard non-porous surfaces.

Disinfectant sprays

Disinfectant sprays are a convenient way to disinfect larger areas quickly and effortlessly. The produced mist can enter small and intricate spaces that are hard to reach with wipes. These advantages come with the downside that the disinfected area must be well ventilated as inhalation of the mist can be harmful. Similar to disinfectant wipes, the application surface should be non-porous and free of dirt and grime. After spraying, the surface must remain wet for several minutes to achieve the desired disinfection as detailed in the product's instructions. Furthermore, rinsing of toys and surfaces that come in contact with food items is mandatory. Commonly known brands include Clorox, Lysol, and Purell.

UVC lights

This category contains devices that emit ultraviolet (UV) light with a wavelength between 200–280 nanometers, also known as the UVC spectrum.[57] This spectrum is particularly well suited to eradicate viruses (and other germs) as it destroys their genetic material. Hospitals have long been using UV light to disinfect whole rooms with mobile UV-light towers, and floor-disinfecting UV-shining robots are roaming hospital hallways at night. While studies proving that UVC light also destroys SARS-CoV-2 are still outstanding, findings for MERS[58] and SARS[59] have shown its efficacy against other coronaviruses. While UVC lights are very promising, they come with the caveat that especially human skin and retina cells (eyes) are also sensitive to this form of radiation as they are the first to get in contact with the light and absorb most of it. This contact can lead to sunburns and even blindness. However, special wavelengths in this spectrum exist that may be harmless to humans (and pets) but still lethal to viruses and microorganisms.[60] This sub-spectrum is named "far-UVC" and should be your first choice when looking to buy a UVC light. Most commercially available UVC lights are not of the far-UVC spectrum, however. They can still be very useful in disinfecting sensitive items, such as mobile phones and other electronics as well as groceries and produce, which are otherwise difficult to disinfect. While UVC devices come in different forms, the most useful products for disinfection of rooms, groceries, and produce are either towers or LED light bulbs that can be used instead of regular light bulbs in ceiling fixtures to disinfect a whole room. Both device types usually come with a remote control to avoid exposure when turned on.

 A word of warning: Not only is UVC light harmful to humans (and pets), but it is likewise dangerous to rely on it when the device does not originate from a trustworthy source, i.e. reputable company. After all, it is difficult to test if a UV lightbulb emits light at the right (UVC) spectrum. Our research on UVC light bulbs offered on major online auction platforms and online retailers showed that many products are not what they are advertised as! We recommend UVC lights only if you have the time to research a prospective product and / or confirmed with the manufacturer that it is indeed designed to emit UVC light. As a rule of thumb: if the product is cheap and you cannot find information on how to contact the manufacturer, do not buy it. Lastly, if you are using UVC lights, ensure that no one, especially no children or pets, have access to the room while the light is switched on. And ensure, as always with electronic products, that the device is approved by a Nationally Recognized Testing Laboratory (NRTL) for your and your household's safety.

Disinfectant application

Frequently touched surfaces

Arguably the biggest benefit to reducing your risk of contracting the virus besides regular handwashing and social distancing is the disinfection of frequently touched surfaces. In particular, those that are shared with members of the public or an infected family member. Some of the most touched shared surfaces include door handles, handrails, shopping carts, keypads, faucets, chairs, tables, trays and pens to name just a few. Regular disinfection with wet wipes or sprays is ideal for these surfaces. Both, disinfectant sprays as well as wipes, come in smaller travel versions that fit in any purse, bag, or pocket for when you are out and about. However, it is often impractical (and could pay you some strange looks from bystanders) to disinfect such surfaces when in public. Therefore, wearing disposable gloves (preferably non-latex to avoid potential allergic reactions) is a good idea. In addition, more and more shops provide disinfectant wipes to clean shopping carts, and medical offices often offer free hand sanitizer. Make use of them when they are provided. Whether or not you wear gloves in public, it is often impossible to avoid touching potentially contaminated items and surfaces when on the go. Mobile phones, wallets, purses, credit cards, steering wheels, and your own face are all good examples of where the virus plans to travel along next, especially once you have it on your hands. This potential contamination issue and the resulting spread of the virus is the key reason why the CDC recommends frequent hand washing with soap and water for at least 20 seconds. As this can also be impracticable at times, carrying (and using) a hand sanitizer with at least 60% alcohol is a great way to reduce this risk. As with disinfectant wipes and sprays, hand sanitizers come in more convenient travel sizes and can be re-filled from a bigger bottle at home.

Mobile phones and other electronics

Mobile phones, tablets, keyboards, TV remotes and other frequently touched electronics are amongst the most germ-laden items around you. On average, by far, dirtier than toilet seats.[61] Due to their sensitivity to liquids, care should be taken when using disinfectant wipes or sprays on these devices. Most disinfectant wipes and sprays also leave unhealthy residues behind that should be wiped off with a damp tissue. A more convenient alternative to off-the-shelf disinfectants is to simply fill the contents of a bottle of rubbing alcohol (70% isopropanol) or 60% ethanol into an empty spray bottle. These liquids evaporate within minutes without leaving any residues behind. However, in rare cases rubbing alcohol and ethanol can fade or dissolve images and text that is printed onto the device. So, test on a small surface area for stability first before using these chemicals on the whole device.

UVC light is a great disinfection method for electronics in general. For mobile phones, there exist specialized disinfectant cases that use UVC light to rid your phone of germs and at the same time protect you from the harmful radiation. Many come with handy features such as charging up your phone while it is being disinfected. Handheld UVC sticks are more versatile but also bear higher risk of accidentally exposing yourself to the harmful light. Handle with caution and follow manufacturer's instructions to reduce your risk.

Mail and Packages

Chances are you have already or are considering ordering essential items through online stores to get them directly delivered to your doorstep. This is a great way to avoid the contact with potentially infected individuals in grocery stores and - in particular - cash register lines. Unfortunately, however, ordering food and other items for delivery is not without risk either. Despite our highly digitized world, physical products do still go through many hands before they arrive at the end consumer. It is not uncommon for products to be handled by dozens of people during assembly, quality control, packaging, business-to-business shipping, warehousing, labeling, and delivery to end consumer. Every time a human handles the product there is a chance for surface contamination. To make it worse, a recent study found that the virus can stay viable on typical surfaces, such as plastic and cardboard for days.[62] The same holds true for mail that is delivered to your mailbox. While the CDC and WHO have stated that the risk of infection through mail is low,[63] you might want to decide for your family to not take any chances and disinfect anything new entering your home.

To do that, you can simply wait until the virus naturally disintegrates by leaving the items outside the house or in the garage (for recommended waiting time see study referred to above). Alternatively, you can disinfect your mail. Start by wearing disposable gloves and a face mask before handling any mail or packages and open them outside of your home, if possible. This will not only limit the exposure of others living with you to potential foreign contaminants from the mail, but also allows you to dispose of the cardboard and envelopes before returning inside. For mail, start by opening all envelopes and placing the contents on one pile. Since letters are usually sensitive to liquids, disinfection with wipes or sprays is not recommended. The ideal method is disinfection through UVC light. However, if you do not have a UVC light, consider taking pictures of the letters and then dispose of them in an outside recycle bin along with the envelopes prior to returning inside. Critically important mail can be placed in a Ziplock bag and brought inside after disinfection with wet wipes. For packages, start by spraying or wiping the box with disinfectants. After opening, continue to either spray or wipe down all items contained within and place them into a clean bag or basket. If you have a UVC light, you can alternatively disinfect the items by placing them into a dedicated room (or preferably the garage) and exposing them to the UV radiation according to the manufacturer's instructions. Rotate the items (while the UV light is off) intermittently to disinfect all sides. Prior to returning to the inside of your home, dispose of your gloves into an outside trash bin and wash hands with soap and water for at least 20 seconds once you've returned inside.

Groceries

Groceries are usually going through quite a journey until they end up on the supermarket shelf. Various intermediaries and distributors in addition to the actual transportation companies move groceries from the production site around the country. And this gets even worse for imported food, which accounts for 15% of the total consumed food in the US.[64] Each step in this food supply chain has the potential to introduce contamination. In addition, shoppers frequently touch products for example to check the nutrition facts before deciding to put the item back on the shelf. Hence, making sure your groceries are not contaminated makes sense, especially if you live in hard-hit areas, such as New York. With non-perishable items, you can simply wait until the virus naturally disintegrates by simply leaving the items outside the house or in the garage for at least three days.[62] Since most groceries are wrapped in plastic, wiping or spraying them with disinfectants is a labor intensive activity but can be a worthwhile option.

 Be sure to only treat completely sealed products this way to not contaminate your food with disinfectant chemicals. For example, bread and other bakery items often come in semipermeable plastic bags for air and moisture circulation.

Frozen products can be treated the same as their thawed counterparts as there is no evidence that the virus is inactivated by low temperatures.[65]

If you already have a UVC light or are willing to invest some money to stop having to wipe down dozens of grocery items by hand, you are in luck. Simply lay out your groceries around a UVC source, such as a tower or under a bulb and let the light do its job. This should of course be done in a separate room or the garage to avoid human exposure to the light. Shifting the items intermittently guarantees the disinfection from to all sides.

Produce

Fresh produce is arguably the hardest category to properly disinfect and at the same time perhaps more prone to transmitting the virus than packaged groceries. This is due to it usually not being wrapped, is often touched, and the fact that it can be eaten raw. It is not recommended to use soap or chemical disinfectants due to the risk of introducing harmful residues into your body when not completely and thoroughly rinsed under running water. In the absence of a UVC light, a good option to reduce potential viral load is to rinse the produce under water and let it dry completely. If you are still concerned, combine that with a three-day waiting period before consumption.[62] Cooking the food will also drastically reduce the viability of any potential viruses.[66] As with groceries, the most convenient disinfection method is through UVC light, which is also often used in commercial disinfection of fruits and vegetables.[57]

Cloths, towels rugs & drapes

Any porous items that can be put into the laundry can be disinfected through machine washing with a regular laundry detergent on the highest temperature setting that will not ruin the fabric (the hotter the better). Specialized laundry additives, such as "Lysol Laundry Sanitizer" exist that are designed to kill germs and may be worthwhile to use in addition, especially if you are caring for an infected family member. For those with skin sensitivities, consider using detergents that are hypoallergenic and use natural or organic ingredients, or consult with your licensed medical provider for proper guidance. When drying in a dryer machine, it is often recommended for those with skin sensitivities to avoid use of anti-static dryer sheets.

Carpets, couches, car seats & mattresses

For porous surfaces that cannot be laundered we found a disinfectant spray to be the most suitable option. It should be noted that most disinfectant sprays are not designed for porous surfaces, but they are probably still your best bet. Due to the contained chemicals in the spray, some fabrics might react with discoloration to the treatment. Therefore, always try the spray on a small hidden spot first before applying it to the rest. If you own a carpet cleaner or if it is available for rent in your area, you can use a disinfectant carpet shampoo or experiment with using disinfectant laundry additive or disinfectant upholstery cleaner as shampoo. If you have a skin sensitivity and are concerned with skin contact with these surfaces upon use of carpet shampoos and cleaners, consider hypoallergenic products and/or those that use natural or organic ingredients. Consult with your licensed medical provider for proper guidance if needed.

Dishes and silverware

Despite that most restaurants have closed for dine-ins, you might find yourself eating in a hospital cafeteria or other institution that is still open. It might be surprising, but the risk of getting infected with the virus through dishes and silverware (or food for that matter) that are provided by a properly registered and certified restaurants is very low. This is because the restaurant industry has already strict guidelines in place that are designed to minimize the spread of pathogens, including viruses. If you are still concerned, you can always bring your own plate and utensils. More realistically however, this becomes a real problem when you are caring for an infected family member and dishes and silverware are shared in the household. In this instance it is critically important to properly disinfect used dishware by running it through a dishwasher on the hottest possible temperature setting. It is generally a good idea to have a set of dedicated dishware for the infected family member. If no well-functioning dishwasher is available in your household, consider using disposable plates and utensils for the infected. If that is also problematic, hand washing using disposable gloves and hot soapy water is the next best option.

Disinfection of face masks

With the current shortage of manufactured face masks, it is only natural to think about disinfecting and re-using them. However, despite hospitals with specialized professional equipment resorting to this strategy to manage the shortage of protective masks, it is a different story for the general public.

 Attempting to disinfect and reuse disposable or single-use masks is not recommended and can do more harm than good. If there is no better alternative, always contact the manufacturer of your particular model first, to find out if and how it can be properly disinfected and/or re-used.

Here are some recommendations on what definitely not to do if you find yourself in a situation where you have no other choice than to disinfect and re-use a disposable mask.

Do not wash N95-type respirators or surgical masks

Washing regular N95-type respirators or surgical masks by hand or machine can cause damage to the microfiber structure of the filter. This will allow more particles to pass through the filter and reduce its protectiveness. Furthermore, it will also deactivate the electrostatic filtration effects of N95-type respirators.

Do not microwave any type of face masks

While there has been evidence that certain viruses can be inactivated quite efficiently with microwaves,[67,68] the potential risks are just not worth it. For starters, many masks contain hidden metal parts that should never be microwaved and can cause fires. Attempting to take these parts out prior to microwaving will most likely destroy the mask. Also, the duration and power of the microwave radiation is important to achieve proper inactivation. This is difficult to re-create for each of the various microwaves out there. Microwaves are also not designed to be run "dry" (without content that absorbs the energy, such as liquids or food). Running it with a mask inside could damage the device, melt mask components or even set them on fire.[69]

Do not use disinfectants on any type of face masks

This may sound counter intuitive, but disinfectant sprays and wipes can contain harsh chemicals and moisture that can damage the microfiber structure of the filter tissue, leading to reduced filter efficiency. They also leave potentially harmful residues behind. Even if they evaporate residue-free like ethanol or rubbing-alcohol, many masks rely on a static electric charge to trap fine particles. This protective mechanism is removed when soaking or spraying with these products.

Now that we know what not to do, here are some strategies that we found during our research and that we have used ourselves to disinfect masks for reuse when there was no better alternative.

Wait for the virus to lose viability

The easiest method to reuse a face mask is to simply store it in a breathable container, such as a paper bag and let it sit for at least two to three days. This is the timeframe after which the virus has generally lost viability.[62,70] However, humidity and temperature play an important role. The higher the temperature and relative humidity, the faster the closely related SARS virus loses viability, a study showed.[71] Therefore, storing the bag containing the used mask in a safe (away from pets and kids), warm and humid place is likely to maximize the virus' natural degradation process.

If you are lucky enough to have multiple masks available, rotate them so that there is always one available. As with all disinfection advice, wear disposable gloves, a face mask and eye protection if available and wash your hands frequently when handling potentially contaminated items.

Boil homemade face masks

Unlike manufactured disposable face masks, homemade masks from the recommended materials, such as cotton can be disinfected by boiling them in water. Note that boiling cotton for the first time can lead to significant shrinkage of the fabric. Therefore, if you plan to disinfect your homemade masks through boiling, boil the fabric before making the mask. Like boiling, there are also experts that recommend ironing with hot steam for disinfection.

Use UVC light and heat

If you only have one mask or need to reuse masks more frequently, a combination of UVC light exposure and subsequent heating can be used. This procedure mimics processes that are used in hospitals, which collect, disinfect, and reuse N95-type respirators several times over to cope with the lack of new masks.[72,73] Assuming you have an adequate UVC light, place the mask close to it and expose it for at least one hour, intermittently rotating it so that all sides receive exposure. Subsequently, place the mask into an oven and heat it to 150–160 degrees Fahrenheit (65–71 degrees Celsius) for another hour. UVC light can be highly effective in disinfecting N95-type masks and mask surfaces in particular,[74,75,76,77,78] but it does not penetrate efficiently into deeper layers of masks, especially those that are made of multiple thick layers. The subsequent heat treatment is intended to inactivate any remaining viruses, also those trapped in deeper layers.

You can store a properly dried and disinfected mask in a closed container, such as a paper or Ziplock bag for future use.

Sewing patterns, size chart and further designs

Sewing patterns

For the improved and advanced sewed masks, we have provided sewing patterns for DIN A4 and US-letter paper sizes. When printing, please ensure you use the actual print size settings on your printer (do not scale or fit to printer margins) and test the printed patterns by measuring the test square to ensure your printer did not alter the dimensions. The folding mask and the simple sewed mask do not require any patterns, as the cut outs are just squares. Please refer to the chart below for size references.

Note: On certain devices it can be difficult or impossible to open the links to the sewing pattern and other links detailed below. To get easy access to all sewing pattern in these cases, we included this QR-code. Simply scan it with the camera app on your mobile phone and select the desired PDFs or links from the newly opened website. If you have any difficulties at all, simply write us an email to contact@ceratul.com and we will be happy to email the PDFs to you.

Sewing patterns for the improved sewed mask with and without filter

Link to the sewing patterns for kids size DIN A4 / Letter:
- http://ceratul.com/fmm1us/sewing_pattern_improved_kids_DIN_A4.pdf
- http://ceratul.com/fmm1us/sewing_pattern_improved_kids_US_letter.pdf

Link to the sewing patterns for small size DIN A4 / Letter:
- http://ceratul.com/fmm1us/sewing_pattern_improved_small_DIN_A4.pdf
- http://ceratul.com/fmm1us/sewing_pattern_improved_small_US_letter.pdf

Link to the sewing patterns for medium size DIN A4 / Letter:
- http://ceratul.com/fmm1us/sewing_pattern_improved_medium_DIN_A4.pdf
- http://ceratul.com/fmm1us/sewing_pattern_improved_medium_US_letter.pdf

Link to the sewing patterns for large size DIN A4 / Letter:
- http://ceratul.com/fmm1us/sewing_pattern_improved_large_DIN_A4.pdf
- http://ceratul.com/fmm1us/sewing_pattern_improved_large_US_letter.pdf

Sewing patterns for the advanced sewed mask

Additional to the above designs, we have developed an even more advanced face mask design. This design requires more sophisticated sewing skills but its build process generally follows the steps outlined for the improved mask. We have compiled a condensed instruction sheet for this advanced sewed face mask that is available for download along with the sewing patterns below.

Link to the sewing instructions for the advanced mask:
- http://ceratul.com/fmm1us/sewing_pattern_advanced_instructions.pdf

Link to the sewing patterns for kids size DIN A4 / Letter:
- http://ceratul.com/fmm1us/sewing_pattern_advanced_kids_DIN_A4.pdf
- http://ceratul.com/fmm1us/sewing_pattern_advanced_kids_US_letter.pdf

Link to the sewing patterns for small size DIN A4 / Letter:
- http://ceratul.com/fmm1us/sewing_pattern_advanced_small_DIN_A4.pdf
- http://ceratul.com/fmm1us/sewing_pattern_advanced_small_US_letter.pdf

Link to the sewing patterns for medium size DIN A4 / Letter:
- http://ceratul.com/fmm1us/sewing_pattern_advanced_medium_DIN_A4.pdf
- http://ceratul.com/fmm1us/sewing_pattern_advanced_medium_US_letter.pdf

Link to the sewing patterns for large size DIN A4 / Letter:
- http://ceratul.com/fmm1us/sewing_pattern_advanced_large_DIN_A4.pdf
- http://ceratul.com/fmm1us/sewing_pattern_advanced_large_US_letter.pdf

Size chart for the sewed mask with and without filter

The actual size will vary depending on the form and size of the wearer's head. For kids, the size will greatly vary depending on the age of the kids. Therefore, the below chart can only be used as a reference. Please try the sizes with a test piece of cloth, before starting to sew your mask. You might also have to make several masks and experiment with the sizes, until you find the perfect fit for you.

Size	Cover material	Earpiece	Nosepiece
Kids	5" (13 cm) x 5" (13 cm)	6" (15 cm)	3" (8 cm)
Small	6" (15 cm) x 6" (15 cm)	7" (18 cm)	4" (10 cm)
Medium	7" (18 cm) x 7" (18 cm)	8" (20 cm)	5" (13 cm)
Large	8" (20 cm) x 8" (20 cm)	9" (23 cm)	6" (15 cm)

References to further designs on the internet

Following the outbreak of the coronavirus, there has been a great effort from institutions, but especially from sewers, inventors and community members to provide, mostly free, sewing instructions, patterns and videos. Some of this work is outstanding and has received millions of views. There are also community projects that encourage making of do-it-yourself masks with the purpose to donate them to hospitals, doctors and others in need. We are very impressed with the level of motivation and willingness to help that many of these projects show.

With hundreds of such projects around, we do not want to rate or prioritize any of them, but below is a list of links to further designs and sewing videos that we found useful during our research for this book.

Sewing instructions and sewing patterns from other sources

- https://wholefully.com/fabric-face-mask-donate/
- https://www.instructables.com/id/DIY-Cloth-Face-Mask/
- https://www.craftpassion.com/face-mask-sewing-pattern/
- https://blog.treasurie.com/diy-mask/
- https://sarahmaker.com/how-to-sew-a-surgical-face-mask-for-hospitals-free-pattern/
- https://tianascloset.com/index.php/2020/02/06/face-mask-against-the-coronavirus-epidemic/
- https://so-sew-easy.com/super-simple-face-mask/
- https://hellosewing.com/face-mask-sewing-pattern/

Video sewing instructions from other sources

- https://www.youtube.com/watch?v=uDMEtbL4xaY
- https://www.youtube.com/watch?v=QpnNcCZn0Vg
- https://www.youtube.com/watch?v=3U0W0mxja8E

About the authors

Cheryl Schwientek, MSEM, CEAS, CPT has over 15 years of occupational health and safety experience, including five and a half years of service as an Assistant Safety Coordinator within the Department of Energy's (DOE) Joint Genome Institute (JGI). She attained her Master's of Science in Environmental Management at the University of San Francisco and a Bachelor's of Science degree in Environmental Health from the University of California at Berkeley. She is also a Certified Ergonomics Assessment Specialist and Certified Personal Fitness Trainer. Cheryl additionally acquired professional certificates in both Worker Safety and Health from the University of California at Davis and in Human Resources Management from the California State University of East Bay. She is now the Program Manager of Office Ergonomics and Health, Safety, and Environment (HSE) at a leading, global consulting firm in injury prevention and workplace health and currently specializes in Site Safety Audits, Job Hazard (or Safety) Analyses, Workplace Health and Safety Programs, Compliance Consultation, and Office Ergonomics.

Patrick Schwientek holds a PhD in Genome Research of Industrial Microorganisms, M.Sc. in Genome Based Systems Biology and a B.Sc. in Bioinformatics. He previously worked for the US Department of Energy's Joint Genome Institute where he studied the genetic code of novel bacteriophages[79] (viruses that infect bacteria) among other things.[80] He continued microbial research at Bayer, before founding his own startup, which is on a mission to end oral diseases through the targeted supplementation of beneficial bacteria.

Moritz von Butler holds a B.A. in European Studies with specialization in International Management and is a certified Lean Six Sigma Master Black Belt, as well as a certified Project Management Professional (PMP). He is a program manager with strong innovation, change and Operational Excellence background, currently focusing on digital product design, user experience design and digitalization. Moritz has a young family with three toddlers and is a member of his local city council.

For this book, Cheryl, Patrick and Moritz partnered with a cloth designer and sewing pattern maker, as well as with an experienced seamstress to derive our face mask designs.

Our spouses and extended families helped to test, design and sew many of the masks.

References

Literature

1. COVID-19 Map. Johns Hopkins Coronavirus Resource Center https://coronavirus.jhu.edu/map.html.
2. Report 12 - The global impact of COVID-19 and strategies for mitigation and suppression. Imperial College London http://www.imperial.ac.uk/medicine/departments/school-public-health/infectious-disease-epidemiology/mrc-global-infectious-disease-analysis/covid-19/report-12-global-impact-covid-19/.
3. Remarks by President Trump, Vice President Pence, and Members of the Coronavirus Task Force in Press Briefing. The White House https://www.whitehouse.gov/briefings-statements/remarks-president-trump-vice-president-pence-members-coronavirus-task-force-press-briefing-14/.
4. Sandford, A. Coronavirus: Half of humanity on lockdown in 90 countries. euronews https://www.euronews.com/2020/04/02/coronavirus-in-europe-spain-s-death-toll-hits-10-000-after-record-950-new-deaths-in-24-hou (2020).
5. High Anxiety in America Over COVID-19. Medscape http://www.medscape.com/viewarticle/927711.
6. Manskar, N. Coronavirus crisis puts 17 million Americans out of work in three weeks. New York Post https://nypost.com/2020/04/09/more-than-6-6-million-americans-file-for-unemployment-amid-coronavirus-crisis/ (2020).
7. Rugaber, C. US jobs report shows 16.6M Americans applied for unemployment since coronavirus outbreak. ABC7 San Francisco https://abc7news.com/6089323/ (2020).
8. WHO - Coronavirus disease (COVID-19) advice for the public. https://www.who.int/emergencies/diseases/novel-coronavirus-2019/advice-for-public.
9. Public Health Experts Keep Changing Their Guidance on Whether or Not to Wear Face Masks for Coronavirus. Time https://time.com/5794729/coronavirus-face-masks/.
10. Remarks by President Trump, Vice President Pence, and Members of the Coronavirus Task Force in Press Briefing. The White House https://www.whitehouse.gov/briefings-statements/remarks-president-trump-vice-president-pence-members-coronavirus-task-force-press-briefing-18/.
11. Rey, J. D. Amazon is banning the sale of N95 and surgical masks to the general public. Vox https://www.vox.com/recode/2020/3/17/21183310/amazon-coronavirus-n95-masks-fba-inventory-seller-vendor-restrictions (2020).
12. ashevillejmFollow. DIY Cloth Face Mask. Instructables https://www.instructables.com/id/DIY-Cloth-Face-Mask/.

13. How to sew your own fabric mask. Washington Post https://www.washingtonpost.com/health/2020/04/05/how-sew-your-own-fabric-mask/.

14. What's the Best Material for a Mask for Coronavirus? - The New York Times. https://www.nytimes.com/article/coronavirus-homemade-mask-material-DIY-face-mask-ppe.html.

15. Naming the coronavirus disease (COVID-19) and the virus that causes it. https://www.who.int/emergencies/diseases/novel-coronavirus-2019/technical-guidance/naming-the-coronavirus-disease-(covid-2019)-and-the-virus-that-causes-it.

16. Cascella, M., Rajnik, M., Cuomo, A., Dulebohn, S. C. & Di Napoli, R. Features, Evaluation and Treatment Coronavirus (COVID-19). in StatPearls (StatPearls Publishing, 2020).

17. CDC. Coronavirus Disease 2019 (COVID-19) – Symptoms. Centers for Disease Control and Prevention https://www.cdc.gov/coronavirus/2019-ncov/symptoms-testing/symptoms.html (2020).

18. CDC. Coronavirus Disease 2019 (COVID-19) – What to Do If You Are Sick. Centers for Disease Control and Prevention https://www.cdc.gov/coronavirus/2019-ncov/if-you-are-sick/steps-when-sick.html (2020).

19. Council, N. R. Rapid Expert Consultation on the Possibility of Bioaerosol Spread of SARS-CoV-2 for the COVID-19 Pandemic (April 1, 2020). (2020). doi:10.17226/25769.

20. Li, R. *et al.* Substantial undocumented infection facilitates the rapid dissemination of novel coronavirus (SARS-CoV2). Science (2020) doi:10.1126/science.abb3221.

21. Zhou, P. *et al.* A pneumonia outbreak associated with a new coronavirus of probable bat origin. Nature 579, 270–273 (2020).

22. Lam, T. T.-Y. *et al.* Identifying SARS-CoV-2 related coronaviruses in Malayan pangolins. Nature 1–6 (2020) doi:10.1038/s41586-020-2169-0.

23. Andersen, K. G., Rambaut, A., Lipkin, W. I., Holmes, E. C. & Garry, R. F. The proximal origin of SARS-CoV-2. Nature Medicine 1–3 (2020) doi:10.1038/s41591-020-0820-9.

24. Memish, Z. A. *et al.* Middle East Respiratory Syndrome Coronavirus in Bats, Saudi Arabia - Volume 19, Number 11—November 2013 - Emerging Infectious Diseases journal - CDC. doi:10.3201/eid1911.131172.

25. CDC. Coronavirus Disease 2019 (COVID-19) – Prevention & Treatment. Centers for Disease Control and Prevention https://www.cdc.gov/coronavirus/2019-ncov/prevent-getting-sick/prevention.html (2020).

26. Resnick, B. Why Covid-19 is worse than the flu, in one chart. Vox https://www.vox.com/science-and-health/2020/3/18/21184992/coronavirus-covid-19-flu-comparison-chart (2020).

27. Cuomo refutes Trump, insists NY needs up to 40,000 ventilators: 'I operate on facts' - syracuse.com. https://www.syracuse.com/coronavirus/2020/03/cuomo-refutes-trump-insists-ny-needs-up-to-40000-ventilators-i-operate-on-facts.html.

28. CDC. Coronavirus Disease 2019 (COVID-19) – Groups at Higher Risk for Severe Illness. Centers for Disease Control and Prevention

https://www.cdc.gov/coronavirus/2019-ncov/need-extra-precautions/groups-at-higher-risk.html (2020).

29. Howard, J. To help stop coronavirus, everyone should be wearing face masks. The science is clear | Jeremy Howard. The Guardian (2020).
30. Milton, D. K., Fabian, M. P., Cowling, B. J., Grantham, M. L. & McDevitt, J. J. Influenza Virus Aerosols in Human Exhaled Breath: Particle Size, Culturability, and Effect of Surgical Masks. PLOS Pathogens 9, e1003205 (2013).
31. Davies, A. *et al.* Testing the efficacy of homemade masks: would they protect in an influenza pandemic? Disaster Med Public Health Prep 7, 413–418 (2013).
32. Full article: Effect of Particle Size on the Performance of an N95 Filtering Facepiece Respirator and a Surgical Mask at Various Breathing Conditions. https://www.tandfonline.com/doi/full/10.1080/02786826.2013.829209.
33. Austria makes masks compulsory as protection debate shifts. https://www.ft.com/content/f68f3063-5024-4654-9389-bcc7ee1efd8e.
34. Wong, T. Why some countries wear face masks and others don't. BBC News (2020).
35. U.S. Surgeon General (@Surgeon_General) / Twitter 'Seriously people, STOP BUYING MASKS'. Twitter https://twitter.com/surgeon_general.
36. CDC. Coronavirus Disease 2019 (COVID-19) - Recommendation Regarding the Use of Cloth Face Coverings, Especially in Areas of Significant Community-Based Transmission. Centers for Disease Control and Prevention https://www.cdc.gov/coronavirus/2019-ncov/prevent-getting-sick/cloth-face-cover.html (2020).
37. CDC - Recommended Guidance for Extended Use and Limited Reuse of N95 Filtering Facepiece Respirators in Healthcare Settings - NIOSH Workplace Safety and Health Topic. https://www.cdc.gov/niosh/topics/hcwcontrols/recommendedguidanceextuse.html (2020).
38. Coronavirus masks explainer. https://view.ceros.com/business-insider-editorial/coronavirus-masks-explainer.
39. Coronavirus: demand for face masks creates shortfall for those in real need. UN News https://news.un.org/en/story/2020/02/1056942 (2020).
40. US accused of 'piracy' over mask 'confiscation'. BBC News (2020).
41. Countries race to limit or ban mask and ventilator exports. Marketplace https://www.marketplace.org/2020/03/30/countries-race-to-limit-ban-exports-of-masks-ventilators-other-gear/ (2020).
42. 'A real cash printer' - Chinese mask producers meet global demand. Industry Europe https://industryeurope.com/api/content/505314d4-7021-11ea-95f1-1244d5f7c7c6/ (2020).
43. March 2, J. A. C. N., 2020 & Pm, 6:30. Coronavirus may infect up to 70% of world's population, expert warns. https://www.cbsnews.com/news/coronavirus-infection-outbreak-worldwide-virus-expert-warning-today-2020-03-02/.
44. How long will the COVID-19 pandemic last? - Health - ABC News. https://www.abc.net.au/news/health/2020-03-20/coronavirus-covid19-pandemic-how-long-will-it-last/12043196.
45. Face Mask Makers Expect Demand To Stay Strong After Coronavirus Subsides. https://www.forbes.com/sites/ralphjennings/2020/02/27/face-mask-makers-expect-demand-to-stay-strong-after-coronavirus-subsides/#cc9428a68f26.

46. Seller Spike: Cost Of Surgical Masks Surges Amid Coronavirus Fears – CBS Dallas / Fort Worth. https://dfw.cbslocal.com/2020/02/26/seller-spike-cost-of-surgical-masks-surges-amid-coronavirus-fears/.
47. Coronavirus and Important Things to Know About Airborne Particles. https://www.filtrete.com/wps/portal/en_US/3M/filtrete/home-tips/full-story/~/coronavirus-and-important-things-to-know-about-airborne-particles/?storyid=d69e7735-c02c-46d2-9c8a-ae23372934ac.
48. News, A. B. C. From scarves to HEPA filters, what kind of face covering is your best bet against coronavirus? ABC News https://abcnews.go.com/Health/scarves-hepa-filters-kind-face-covering-best-bet/story?id=70058603.
49. Robertson, P. What Are The Best Materials for Making DIY Masks? Smart Air Filters https://smartairfilters.com/en/blog/best-materials-make-diy-face-mask-virus/ (2020).
50. When and how to use masks. https://www.who.int/emergencies/diseases/novel-coronavirus-2019/advice-for-public/when-and-how-to-use-masks.
51. Bae, S. *et al.* Effectiveness of Surgical and Cotton Masks in Blocking SARS–CoV-2: A Controlled Comparison in 4 Patients. Ann Intern Med (2020) doi:10.7326/M20-1342.
52. Surgent, G. Surgent General explains simple mask assembly. https://www.cdc.gov/wcms/video/low-res/coronavirus/2020/37637620200403_SG-Mask-v2.mp4.
53. CDC. Coronavirus Disease 2019 (COVID-19) – Caring for Children. Centers for Disease Control and Prevention https://www.cdc.gov/coronavirus/2019-ncov/daily-life-coping/children.html (2020).
54. expert reaction to reports that the (previously reported) pet dog in Hong Kong has repeatedly tested 'weak positive' for COVID-19 virus | Science Media Centre. https://www.sciencemediacentre.org/expert-reaction-to-reports-that-the-previously-reported-pet-dog-in-hong-kong-has-repeatedly-tested-weak-positive-for-covid-19-virus/.
55. Questions and Answers on the COVID-19: OIE - World Organisation for Animal Health. https://www.oie.int/en/scientific-expertise/specific-information-and-recommendations/questions-and-answers-on-2019novel-coronavirus/.
56. CDC. Coronavirus Disease 2019 (COVID-19) - CDC Statement for Healthcare Personnel on Hand Hygiene during the Response to the International Emergence of COVID-19. Centers for Disease Control and Prevention https://www.cdc.gov/coronavirus/2019-ncov/hcp/hand-hygiene.html (2020).
57. Kim, S.-J., Kim, D.-K. & Kang, D.-H. Using UVC Light-Emitting Diodes at Wavelengths of 266 to 279 Nanometers To Inactivate Foodborne Pathogens and Pasteurize Sliced Cheese. Appl Environ Microbiol 82, 11–17 (2015).
58. Keil, S. D., Bowen, R. & Marschner, S. Inactivation of Middle East respiratory syndrome coronavirus (MERS-CoV) in plasma products using a riboflavin-based and ultraviolet light-based photochemical treatment. Transfusion 56, 2948–2952 (2016).
59. Duan, S.-M. *et al.* Stability of SARS coronavirus in human specimens and environment and its sensitivity to heating and UV irradiation. Biomed. Environ. Sci. 16, 246–255 (2003).
60. Welch, D. *et al.* Far-UVC light: A new tool to control the spread of airborne-mediated microbial diseases. Scientific Reports 8, 1–7 (2018).

61. Your Cell Phone Is 10 Times Dirtier Than a Toilet Seat | Time. https://time.com/4908654/cell-phone-bacteria/.
62. van Doremalen, N. *et al.* Aerosol and Surface Stability of SARS-CoV-2 as Compared with SARS-CoV-1. New England Journal of Medicine 0, null (2020).
63. Twilley, N. You've Got Mail. Will You Get the Coronavirus? The New York Times (2020).
64. Nutrition, C. for F. S. and A. FDA Strategy for the Safety of Imported Food. FDA (2020).
65. WHO-COVID-19 Situation Report – 32.
66. Food Safety and Coronavirus: A Comprehensive Guide | The Food Party! | Laura Stec | Palo Alto Online |. https://paloaltoonline.com/blogs/p/2020/03/21/food-safety-and-coronavirus-a-comprehensive-guide.
67. Siddharta, A. *et al.* Inactivation of HCV and HIV by microwave: a novel approach for prevention of virus transmission among people who inject drugs. Sci Rep 6, (2016).
68. Sanborn, M. R., Wan, S. K. & Bulard, R. Microwave sterilization of plastic tissue culture vessels for reuse. Appl Environ Microbiol 44, 960–964 (1982).
69. Fire Safety Tips for Using Microwave Ovens. https://www.ors.od.nih.gov/News/Pages/Using_Microwave_Ovens.aspx.
70. CDC. Coronavirus Disease 2019 (COVID-19) - Environmental Cleaning and Disinfection Recommendations. Centers for Disease Control and Prevention https://www.cdc.gov/coronavirus/2019-ncov/prevent-getting-sick/cleaning-disinfection.html (2020).
71. Chan, K. H. *et al.* The Effects of Temperature and Relative Humidity on the Viability of the SARS Coronavirus. Advances in Virology https://www.hindawi.com/journals/av/2011/734690/ (2011) doi:https://doi.org/10.1155/2011/734690.
72. Scott, T. In hospitals and labs, researchers find ways to clean and reuse masks. https://www.michiganradio.org/post/hospitals-and-labs-researchers-find-ways-clean-and-reuse-masks.
73. Farke, J. N95 Filtering Facepiece Respirator Ultraviolet Germicidal Irradiation (UVGI) Process for Decontamination and Reuse. 19.
74. Lore, M. B., Heimbuch, B. K., Brown, T. L., Wander, J. D. & Hinrichs, S. H. Effectiveness of Three Decontamination Treatments against Influenza Virus Applied to Filtering Facepiece Respirators. Ann Occup Hyg 56, 92–101 (2012).
75. Mills, D., Harnish, D. A., Lawrence, C., Sandoval-Powers, M. & Heimbuch, B. K. Ultraviolet germicidal irradiation of influenza-contaminated N95 filtering facepiece respirators. American Journal of Infection Control 46, e49–e55 (2018).
76. Tseng, C.-C. & Li, C.-S. Inactivation of Viruses on Surfaces by Ultraviolet Germicidal Irradiation. Journal of Occupational and Environmental Hygiene 4, 400–405 (2007).
77. Viscusi, D. J., Bergman, M. S., Eimer, B. C. & Shaffer, R. E. Evaluation of Five Decontamination Methods for Filtering Facepiece Respirators. Ann Occup Hyg 53, 815–827 (2009).
78. Lindsley, W. G. *et al.* Effects of Ultraviolet Germicidal Irradiation (UVGI) on N95 Respirator Filtration Performance and Structural Integrity. Journal of Occupational and Environmental Hygiene 12, 509–517 (2015).

79. Ivanova, N. N. *et al.* Stop codon reassignments in the wild. Science 344, 909–913 (2014).
80. Rinke, C. *et al.* Insights into the phylogeny and coding potential of microbial dark matter. Nature advance online publication, (2013).

Pictures

Photo of ultrastructural morphology exhibited by coronaviruses, by CDC, on Unsplash, licensed under Unsplash license, https://unsplash.com/photos/k0KRNtqcjfw

The warning icon used in this book made was by surang from www.flaticon.com

www.ingramcontent.com/pod-product-compliance
Lightning Source LLC
Chambersburg PA
CBHW051429150726
48000CB00005B/2019